I. INTRODUCTION

A. MAJOR RESEARCH QUESTION

Cyber threats make the headlines daily, from attacks on critical infrastructure to personal identity theft. Government agencies, businesses, and individuals alike have become more dependent on technology, and the desire and need for interconnectedness has led to increasing network vulnerability affecting both government and private sectors. Policymakers and cyber experts continue to push for legislation that encourages private companies to participate voluntarily in information sharing programs to better guard against cybercrime and espionage. Recognizing both government and private sectors alone lack the capabilities to defend against cyber threats,[1] President Obama, under Executive Order 13636 and Presidential Policy Directive (PPD) 21, directed several government agencies, with the Department of Homeland Security (DHS) taking the lead, to establish a more robust and resilient cybersecurity alliance that encourages information-sharing partnerships with private sector owners and operators in charge of protecting U.S. critical infrastructure (CI).

Despite the recent drive for cyber legislation and policies, government agencies and private companies have seemed reluctant to disclose information related to cyber-attacks and threats with one another. This thesis asks why do cybersecurity information-sharing problems exist between the government and the private sector? In doing so, it also investigates how public-private partnerships (PPPs) respond to these problems to satisfy national cybersecurity needs; and reveals these underlying issues for policymakers to consider when shaping policies that encourage an open dialog between the public and private sector.

---

[1] "Fact Sheet: Executive Order 13636 and Presidential Policy Directive (PPD)-21," Department of Homeland Security, March 2013, http://www.dhs.gov/publication/fact-sheet-eo-13636-improving-critical-infrastructure-cybersecurity-and-ppd-21-critical.

B. IMPORTANCE OF RESEARCH

Efforts to foster and increase information sharing have recently emerged from both the government and private sectors. Two examples that emanated from EO 13636 are the National Institute of Standards and Technology's (NIST) Framework version 1.0 (shaped by both private industry and government),[2] and the Department of Homeland Security's (DHS) Critical Infrastructure Cyber Community Volunteer Program (C^{3}VP).[3] The Framework promises to improve resiliency and encourage discussion of best practices for managing cybersecurity risk; CV^{3}P encourages private businesses to adopt the Cybersecurity Framework. However, both programs——still in their infancy——are voluntary; there is much debate over whether such programs will be effective; for example, some have critiqued how the language in the EO only specifies the directional flow of information from the private sector to government agencies.[4]

Cybersecurity experts, lobbyists, and sector-specific agencies (SSAs) of critical infrastructure argue the need for better legislation and guidance that not only facilitates collaboration from both private and government agencies, but also provides liability protection against litigation for disclosure while sharing information and responding to cyber-threats.[5] For example, the Department of Treasury (SSA in charge of protecting the financial services sector) recognized the need for more public-private collaboration in improving cybersecurity to the U.S. financial sector—listed as one of four strategic

---

[2] "Framework for Improving Critical Infrastructure Cybersecurity: Version 1.0," National Institute Standards and Technology, February 12, 2014, http://www.nist.gov/cyberframework/upload/ cybersecurity-framework-021214.pdf.

[3] "Critical Infrastructure Cyber Community Voluntary Program," United States Computer Emergency Readiness Team, Department of Homeland Security, accessed May 27, 2014, http://www.us-cert.gov/ccubedvp.

[4] Veronica A. Chinn, Furches, Lee T., and Woodward, Barian A., "Information- Sharing with the Private Sector," National Defense University Press, April 1, 2014, http://ndupress.ndu.edu/Media/News/NewsArticleView/tabid/7849/Article/8464/jfq-73-information-sharing-with-the-private-sector.aspx.

[5] Ryan Tracy, "Cybersecurity Legislation Gets Push From Financial Firms," *The Wall Street Journal*, Law Blog, November 13, 2013, http://blogs.wsj.com/law/2013/11/13/cybersecurity-legislation-gets-push-from-financial-firms/.

objectives in safeguarding the financial system against cybersecurity threats in the department's Strategic Plan FY 2014–2017.[6]

Current literature on cyber information sharing focuses on endorsing cybersecurity legislation, policies, and laws that encourage or even mandate government-private sector partnerships. Some argue that government declassification and disclosure of known cyber threats to private companies is the answer,[7] while others argue that the answer rests in the private sector sharing timely cyber threat information with government agencies.[8] Despite these conventional arguments, the bulk of current literature lacks discussion of other possibilities. A more focused approach that examines similar public-private relationships within individual CI sectors could reveal further motivations or explanations that could add value to the existing body of knowledge on cybersecurity issues between the government and private sector. This thesis attempts to discover the deeper underlying issues that inhibit public-private cooperation.

C. LITERATURE REVIEW

The concept of public-private partnerships (PPP) dates back to the Colonial period in North America when John Winthrop, Jr. established a series of pharmaceutical laboratories, which led to the idea that government agencies could utilize private businesses to not only advance the progress of science, but also benefit society.[9] PPPs—situations in which government agencies interact with private companies—are unique to other government-private associations in that they both share in the resources, risks, and

---

[6] Department of Treasury, *Department of the Treasury FY 2014–2017 Strategic Plan*, 32, http://www.treasury.gov/about/budget-performance/strategic-plan/Documents/2014–2017US_TreasuryStrategicPlan.pdf.

[7] Kelly Riddell, "Ex-FBI Official: Intel Agencies Don't Share Cyber threats that Endanger Companies," *The Washington Times,* May 11, 2014, http://www.washingtontimes.com/news/2014/may/11/intel-agencies-dont-share-cyber-threats-that-could/?page=all.

[8] James B. Comey, "The FBI and the Private Sector: Closing the Gap in Cyber Security," Speech, February 26, 2014, http://www.fbi.gov/news/speeches/the-fbi-and-the-private-sector-closing-the-gap-in-cyber-security.

[9] Thomas Cellucci, "Innovative Public-Private Partnerships: Pathway to Effectively Solving Problems," Department of Homeland Security, July 2010, 4, http://www.dhs.gov/xlibrary/assets/st_innovative_public_private_partnerships_0710_version_2.pdf.

costs of delivering a service to the public.[10] A more complete definition of PPPs is provided in Chapter III: Public-Private Partnerships in Cybersecurity. Today, many, particularly in the Executive Branch, still believe in that same concept and submit that fostering an information sharing alliance between government agencies and private businesses that share in both costs and benefits is the best course of action to defend against cyber-related attacks.

To understand the significance of the lack of cybersecurity information sharing between public and private entities, it is necessary to find a place in time when cybersecurity became a major issue. The prevailing literature on cybersecurity tends to emerge around 2006 as the landmark year when we begin to see a significant rise in cyber incidents.[11] This steep upsurge in cyber-related attacks and threats highlighted the need for immediate cybersecurity reform. Recognizing that the private sector controls the majority of our nation's critical infrastructure, the president released Executive Order 13636 in an effort to streamline cybersecurity regulations across both public and private agencies to foster a more resilient cyber defense.[12]

Over the past several years (before and after the release of EO 13636), government officials and private sector leaders alike have pressed for more public-private collaboration to increase cybersecurity across all sixteen sectors of CI. Despite this widespread urgency, policymakers have found difficulty in drafting legislation that not only protects our national infrastructure, but also balances security and privacy.[13] The concept of cooperation between government agencies and the private sector continues to be a controversial issue.

---

[10] Cellucci, "Innovative Public-Private Partnerships," 4.

[11] "Significant Cyber Events," Center for Strategic and International Studies, last modified March 10, 2014, http://csis.org/files/publication/140310_Significant_Cyber_Incidents_Since_2006.pdf.

[12] Executive Order no. 13636, *Improving Critical Infrastructure Cybersecurity*, DCPD-2013000 91, February 19, 2013, http://www.gpo.gov/fdsys/pkg/FR-2013-02-19/pdf/2013-03915.pdf.

[13] Chertoff group has noted in a recent Cybersecurity Presentation, "Over 50 different pieces of Legislation introduced in the past two years." Ben Beeson, Gerald Ferguson, and Mark Weatherford, "Implementation of the Cybersecurity Executive Order," slide 6, November 13, 2013, http://chertoffgroup.com/events.php.

In 2010, the U.S. Government Accountability Office (GAO) released a report upon Congressional request to determine cyber-related PPP expectations from the stakeholder's perspective—and to evaluate the degree those expectations were being satisfied. Utilizing both public and private employees, the GAO distributed surveys, conducted interviews, and analyzed relevant policies across five CI sectors that rely heavily on cyber assets to support operations: Communications, Defense Industry Base, Energy, Banking and Finance, and Information Technology.[14] In 2012, the White House released Presidential Policy Directive (PPD-21), which identified and established 16 separate critical infrastructure sectors.[15] Further discussion of PPD-21 is provided in Chapter II.

The GAO found that private sector expectations, such as timely sharing of cyber-related threats from the federal government and granting of security clearances, fell short. Less than one-third of those surveyed reported receiving usable threat information.[16] The report also found that government expectations, such as implementing government recommendations and sensitive information sharing, were also unsatisfactory. For example, some private stakeholders refused to share sensitive information due to government distrust.[17] Although the GAO identifies several inadequacies of cybersecurity PPPs, the report makes only two recommendations: Utilize results to improve on expectations and augment a central point for better information integration.[18] These recommendations lack any real plan of action or guidance for policymakers. Another issue is the scope of the GAO's research, which compared the effectiveness of cybersecurity of five complex CI sectors. While the report's initial findings seem beneficial to improving PPP's within those sectors, such findings cannot be assumed across all sectors of CI. A more focused approach that compares only two or three similar

---

[14] David A. Powner, *Critical Infrastructure Protection: Key Private and Public Cyber Expectations Need to be Consistently Addressed,* United States Government Accountability Office, 2010, 7, http://search.proquest.com/ docview/831086945?accountid=12702.

[15] "Critical Infrastructure Sectors," Department of Homeland Security. accessed December, 15 2014, http://www.dhs.gov/critical-infrastructure-sectors.

[16] Powner, *Critical Infrastructure Protection,* 16.

[17] Ibid., 22.

[18] Ibid., 23–24.

sectors could yield additional answers, produce more accurate and timely results, and utilize fewer resources. Regardless of the report's findings, it does reveal some initial issues facing PPPs and establishes the reference point for further research in answering why a problem exists between government agencies and private companies in sharing cyber-related threat information.

Perhaps the most thorough and recent scholarly work on the topic of cybersecurity information sharing is Forrest Hare's Dissertation on *The Interdependent Nature of National Cyber Security.* He argues the need for cyber related information sharing between both government and private agencies and analyzes the electric power sector's motivations for information sharing as the United States looks to start using new technologies, such as the Smart Grid.[19] Hare also stresses the importance of the private sector's investment in cybersecurity and contribution to public-private information sharing in order to strengthen cyber defenses and increase response time to threats and incidents.[20] Hare's research findings identify several barriers and disincentives of information sharing between government and private agencies within the electric power sector.[21] He also found that additional government regulation over cybersecurity does not pose a negative impact on private sector motivations; however, he discovered that increased regulation would result in a "greater reporting burden and fewer resources devoted to actually improving [cyber] security."[22] Hare further adds that companies might be more willing to invest in more cybersecurity measures if other private sector companies incurred the same costs.

Hare asks two questions. First, in the interest of national security and absent government regulation, what motivations exist that encourage private firms to invest in cybersecurity procedures?[23] Second, how can public-private information sharing offer

---

[19] Forrest B. Hare, "The Interdependent Nature of National Cyber Security: Motivating Private Action for a Public Good" (PhD diss., George Mason University, 2010), 155, Dudley Knox Inter Library Loan: 129484.

[20] Ibid., 184.

[21] Ibid., 205–6.

[22] Ibid., 214.

[23] Ibid., 93.

utility to both parties within the electric power critical infrastructure sector?[24] He also identifies and attempts to prove multiple hypotheses centered on the electric power CI sector. While Hare's work does not evaluate the effectiveness of cybersecurity information sharing between government and private-sector agencies, it does identify the potential of public-private partnerships to directly improve trust and motivation to cooperate while indirectly increasing interaction between both sides.[25] He concludes that, "the private sector needs to have a better understanding of how their actions and inactions are directly related to nation security," further suggesting that additional research that focuses on such factors could aid cybersecurity experts across all sectors of Critical Infrastructure.[26] Hare's extensive research establishes a baseline of knowledge upon which this thesis will attempt to build.

In 2011, five leading cybersecurity associations released a white paper highlighting several cybersecurity achievements resulting from public-private partnerships. The authors base their research on President Obama's 2009 Cyberspace Policy Review (CSPR) and the 2009 National Infrastructure Protection Plan (NIPP). The paper identifies seven key areas of cybersecurity that align with the CSPR, including risk management; information sharing and privacy; and education and awareness. The paper also offers several recommendations to include calling for more transparency and sharing of secret information from the government, and for Congress to amend current surveillance laws tailored for cybersecurity.[27] It also suggests that both government and private agencies develop incentives that encourage voluntary adoption and investment of best security practices and technology within the guidelines of the NIPP framework.[28] Additionally, the paper proposes greater cybersecurity education and awareness training,

---

[24] Hare, "The Interdependent Nature," 185.

[25] Ibid., 222–23.

[26] Ibid., 256.

[27] Business Software Alliance, et al., "Improving our Nation's Cybersecurity Through the Public-Private Partnership: White Paper," March 8, 2011, 17, https://cdt.org/files/pdfs/20110308_cbyersec_paper.pdf.

[28] Ibid., 12.

to include hiring more cyber experts in both public and private agencies.[29] While these recommendations are plausible, they are repetitive of past research findings. Moreover, the paper lacks any discourse to answering why government agencies and private companies seem reluctant to disclose information related to cybersecurity.

One year prior to the release of EO 13636, the United States experienced its largest increase ever in cyber-attacks against critical infrastructure. Although the details behind the sudden hike in cyber awareness were unclear, there were several contributing factors, such as an increase in technology, a surge in sophisticated hackers, and an escalation in probing from other non-allied countries such as Russia and China. [30] James Lewis, Senior Fellow from the Center for Strategic and International Studies (CSIS) noted, "We hit rock bottom on [cybersecurity] in 2010. Then we hit rock bottom in 2011. And we are still at rock bottom," indicating that the United States is becoming increasingly vulnerable to cyber-attacks on critical infrastructure.[31]

The beginning of 2012 brought light to the problem of government's (particularly the Department of Homeland Security's) role in encouraging the private sector to invest in a more robust network security. As cyber-related attacks continued to increase, cyber experts and government officials (including the president) began to push for legislation that not only grants the federal government the authority to begin sharing information with the private sector, but also establishes minimum cybersecurity standards that private companies in charge of operating and protecting critical infrastructure would be required to achieve.[32] John Brennan, who was then President Obama's senior adviser on counterterrorism and homeland security, strongly urged for a more mandated cybersecurity policy versus a voluntary system, and was a large supporter of the proposed Cybersecurity Act of 2012. He highlights how the private sector and government

---

[29] Business Software Alliance, et al., "Improving our Nation's Cybersecurity," 25.

[30] Michael Schmidt, "New Interest in Hacking as Threat to Security," *The New York Times*, March 13, 2012, http://www.nytimes.com/2012/03/14/us/new-interest-in-hacking-as-threat-to-us-security.html?_r=0.

[31] Ibid.

[32] John Brennan, "Time to Protect Against Dangers of Cyberattack," *The Washington Post*, April 15, 2012, http://www.washingtonpost.com/opinions/time-to-protect-against-dangers-ofcyberattack/2012/04/15/gIQAdJP8JT_story.html.

agencies in the past have teamed up to protect critical infrastructure from physical threats, adding "There is no reason we cannot work together in the same way to protect the cybersystems of our critical infrastructure."[33]

President Obama also wrote an op-ed identifying the security gaps that exist from companies that have not adopted more robust cyber defenses. He stressed the necessity for a set of cybersecurity standards developed and executed by both private and government agencies that not only protects our national and economic security, but also protects the privacy and civil liberties of all Americans.[34] Then-National Security Agency (NSA) and U.S. Cyber Command chief General Keith Alexander also voiced his concern over the increase of cyber-related attacks on U.S. Critical Infrastructure and urged for legislation that enables the government to defend private networks against cyber threats—despite deep concerns from private businesses and civil liberty groups over rising costs on network regulation and privacy issues.[35] These views continue to highlight that the drive toward a more secure network that protects critical infrastructure lacks due regard for potential public-private information sharing problems.

While many have argued that PPP's are needed to protect our Nation's Critical Infrastructure Key Resources (CIKR) against cyber-attacks and threats, there are those who have critiqued the Executive's approach to regulating cybersecurity of private industry networks. The year 2012 became a controversial year for cybersecurity legislation, with experts and politicians battling both sides of the argument of empowering DHS to regulate cybersecurity.[36] Prior to the release of EO 13636, three senators (John McCain R-AZ, Kay Hutchison R-TX, and Saxby Chambliss R-GA) expressed their opinion of how the Executive Branch's mandate actually hurts the

---

[33] Brennan, "Time to Protect."

[34] Barack Obama, "Taking the Cyberattack Threat Seriously," *The Wall Street Journal*, July 19, 2012, http://online.wsj.com/news/articles/SB10000872396390444330904577535492693 044650.

[35] David E. Sanger and Eric Schmitt, "Rise is Seen in Cyberattacks Targeting U.S. Infrastructure," *The New York Times,* July 26, 2012, http://www.nytimes.com/2012/07/27/us/ cyberattacks-are-up-national-security-chief-says.html.

[36] Ellen Nakashima, "On Cybersecurity Bill, Battle Lines Forming," *The Washington Post,* February 17, 2012, http://www.washingtonpost.com/blogs/checkpoint-washington/post/ divisions-erupt-over-cybersecurity-bill/2012/02/17/gIQAG348IR_blog.html.

potential for public-private partnerships. They cited antitrust laws and statutory limitations as the legal hurdles discouraging private companies from collaborating in cyber-threat sharing activities with government agencies, stressing that "companies must first check with their lawyers before sharing information for fear of litigation, not just from customers or shareholders but from federal and state governments as well."[37] In rebuttal, they urged the president to release a bipartisan information-sharing bill that grants clear authority to share cyber-threat information between government entities and private companies that includes liability protections in lieu of EO 13636.[38] The three senators, who were ranking Republicans on the Armed Services Committee, also stated that "new statutory protections would drive information sharing and significantly improve our nation's cybersecurity," and strongly felt that such protections would unnecessarily amend existing law. At the time, they believed that the executive order by itself would not be enough to foster a government-private cybersecurity alliance.

While policymakers, cyber experts, and the media debated over cybersecurity legislation and privacy concerns, the impact of PPPs on homeland security issues received little attention. Recognizing the lack of scholarly literature on PPPs and protecting CI from all hazards, including cyber-related threats, Nathan Busch and Austen Givens attempted to fill this gap by presenting their research in an October 2012 edition of *Homeland Security Affairs*. Their work focuses on examining the evolving role of PPPs and discusses the benefits, limitations, challenges, and incentives that PPPs face in protecting the nation from all threats. Because 85% of our nation's CI is under private sector control, the authors stress the need for an alliance between DHS and private sector companies.[39] While only a limited section is dedicated to cybersecurity, the research overall is applicable to all sectors of critical infrastructure.

---

[37] John McCain, Kay Hutchison, and Saxby Chambliss, "No Cybersecurity Executive Order, Please," *The Wall Street Journal*, Sept 4, 2012, http://www.mccain.senate.gov/public/ index.cfm/opinion-editorials?ID=c5083e37–061e-ac3f-8e9b-2594e43f9d2c.

[38] Ibid.

[39] Nathan E. Busch and Austen D. Givens, "Public-Private Partnerships in Homeland Security: Opportunities and Challenges," *Homeland Security Affairs* 8, no. 1 (2012) 3, http://search.proquest.com/docview/1266365905?accountid=12702.

Although the authors highlight the many benefits to PPPs, including building trust and technological innovation, they also address what the previous literature on PPPs seems to lack: potential limitations and challenges. For example, one limitation the authors discuss is how poor management within PPPs can lead to rising costs and failed expectations, such as the Virtual Fence project that DHS ultimately cancelled.[40] Another limitation that previous literature misses is the appearance versus reality problem of PPPs. While businesses may publicly appear to place security as a top priority, secretly, they are more concerned about their bottom line. Private organizations may also appear to share mutual security standards set by the government; however, in reality corporations are more likely to avoid complying with costly security recommendations. Thus, the appearance of public-private cooperation concerning cybersecurity is often less of a reality.[41] The authors also identify another pitfall to government-private sector collaboration in their critique of the Critical Infrastructure Partnership Advisory Council (CIPAC)—an organization within DHS comprised of both government and private businesses that share information to protect CI at the federal level. Despite the council's many contributions to PPPs, some view CIPACs position as "overly government-centric" by siding with the government over private industry concerns.[42] As a result, some private firms may become discouraged if they share information with government agencies but those agencies do not reciprocate in a timely fashion. Busch and Givens conclude that although PPPs within homeland security endure significant challenges and limitations, "future studies will need to examine other critical issues that become relevant as [PPPs] continue."[43] The authors' findings helps establish a baseline of knowledge in government-private sector information sharing issues in which this thesis will attempt to expand upon by exploring current barriers to collaboration within a single CI sector.

The most recent work to date that attempts to assess the status quo of public-private partnerships in securing cyberspace is a comparative analysis conducted by

---

[40]Busch and Givens, "Public-Private Partnerships," 9.

[41] Ibid.

[42] Ibid., 4.

[43] Ibid., 15.

Rachel Nyswander Thomas, Vice President of Government Affairs for the Direct Marketing Association,[44] and published by CSIS. She examined the current (2012) status of cybersecurity PPPs by analyzing several partnership models and offered a few alternatives for policymakers to consider in meeting the nation's cybersecurity expectations.[45] Her research sought to determine the PPP model most suitable in helping secure cyberspace. By analyzing preceding cybersecurity PPPs, Thomas discovered that pressure, coupled with a sense of urgency, is what forced many government and private sector agencies to collaborate rather than using a more systematic approach; based on this finding, she concluded that the field of cybersecurity was mature enough to begin comparing different cybersecurity PPP models.[46] Out of four alternate models, only one met the set criteria determined to provide a more secure cyberspace: a civic switchboard that coordinates public-private cyber information sharing under the direct authority of the Executive Office.[47] Thomas also found that despite the requirement of an ISAC for every CI sector under Presidential Decision Directive (PDD) 63, several CI sectors lack an Information Sharing Analysis Center (ISAC) counterpart—partly due to disagreements between industry leaders as to the necessity of an ISAC investment.[48] One could argue that sectors lacking an ISAC hinder information sharing between government agencies and industry; yet, her research does not fully investigate this issue. While Thomas' contribution helps reinforce the status quo reiterated in previous literature that PPPs remain an integral piece of the cybersecurity puzzle, her research contains one particular weakness—source attribution.

Although her report was initially published in May 2012, Thomas updated it in August 2013. However, the updated report lacks an explanation of the content added or changed—including the extent of change—leaving it up to the reader to hunt for the

---

[44]"Rachel Nyswander Thomas," bio, Direct Marketing Association website, http://thedma.org/dma/rachel-nyswander-thomas/.

[45] Rachel Nyswander Thomas, "Securing Cyberspace Through Public-Private Partnership: A Comparative Analysis of Partnership Models," May 2012, 8, Last updated August 2013 http://csis.org/files/publication/130819_ tech_summary.pdf.

[46] Ibid., 31.

[47] Ibid., 53.

[48] Ibid., 9, 28.

changes using footnotes. More importantly, the facts derived from the personal interviews Thomas conducted over the course of her research might be the most important contribution to the existing literature on PPPs in securing cyberspace; yet, those sources remain anonymous in the report, which makes assessing the credibility of these sources difficult—if not impossible. For example, Thomas states, "only 200 people in the entire financial services sector have a clearance level that would enable them to receive classified information directly from ISAC partners."[49] While this information helps address the issue of the government providing timely security clearances to private-sector owners of CI, the source remains nameless. Similar research that acknowledges reputable sources could yield a more practical and plausible contribution to the existing body of knowledge on cybersecurity PPPs.

Despite an enormous hike in cyber-related attacks, literature concerning cybersecurity and PPPs began to decline in 2013. While journalists, cybersecurity experts, and policymakers stressed the importance of government-private sector collaboration on cybersecurity efforts, scholarly research on the effectiveness of PPPs took a back seat. Days after the release of the EO 13636, FBI Director Robert Mueller stressed the importance of information sharing between the Bureau and other government agencies—to include the private sector. He believed the problem was the lack of urgency in private companies to recognize the seriousness of cyber-related threats. Mueller cited several successful examples of PPP models, including the National Cyber Forensics and Training Alliance (collaboration of law enforcement and private industry); Enduring Security Framework (group of private and government leaders that analyze cyber-related threats); and the FBI's own Domestic Security Alliance Council (consisting of security representatives from all CI and business sectors).[50] These models could serve as potential case studies in helping solve the cybersecurity information-sharing problem. Both the NCFTA and ESF are discussed in Chapter III, Section D: Cybersecurity PPPs in Action.

---

[49] Thomas, "Securing Cyberspace ," 12.

[50] "The Cyber Threat–Planning for the Way Ahead," Federal Bureau of Investigation, February 19, 2013, http://www.fbi.gov/news/stories/2013/february/the-cyber-threat-planning-for-the-way-ahead/the-cyber-threat-planning-for-the-way-ahead.

Within a month of the president's Executive Order, media outlets began reporting that security companies, such as Raytheon and Lockheed Martin, were lobbying for stronger cyber laws that mandated more stringent cybersecurity requirements, in order to boost sales in security products. Meanwhile, the victims of cyber-attacks—banking, communication, and energy sectors—pushed for better liability protection and threat assessments from government agencies.[51] The majority of cybersecurity publicity during 2013 consisted of continual recommendations on policy and ways to increase cyber defenses with very little research into the effectiveness of PPPs. However, retired Rear Admiral and current Cybersecurity Solutions Group Vice President Elizabeth A. Hight cited one particular case where the Department of Energy (DOE) and DHS formed an information-sharing alliance with several different energy companies—highlighting the potential value in using mature partnership models as benchmarks that can measure forward progress in cybersecurity. Hight noted, "[w]hen industry and the public sector are able to access and receive timely, actionable information, better solutions emerge," further arguing that such models establish a standard for other CI sectors to follow.[52]

By now, it should be evident that, despite an obvious increase in cyber-related threats to our nation's CI, government and private entities have been at times both willing and reluctant to forge PPPs that encourage information sharing to enhance cybersecurity. Absent from the current literature is a more focused analysis that examines whether or not similar CI specific agencies enjoy more or less cooperation on cybersecurity matters within their respective private industries. This research adds to the existing body of knowledge by exploring the current barriers to PPPs within the finance sector[53] to help fill the gap between the government's push to increase cyber resiliency and the seemingly

---

[51] Eric Engleman and Jonathan D. Salant, "U.S. Cybersecurity Policy Draws Interest From Companies, Lobbyists," *The Washington Post,* March 24, 2013, http://www.washingtonpost.com/business/economy/us-cybersecurity-policy-draws-interest-from-companies-lobbyists/2013/03/24/916a79f2–9271–11e2-bdea-e32ad90da239_story.html.

[52] Elizabeth A. Hight, "Forging A Public-private Partnership for Cybersecurity: Government, Private Sector Collaboration Key to Forward-looking Security," Washington Technology, April 30, 2013, http://washingtontechnology.com/articles/2013/04/30/insights-hight-cyber-collaboration.aspx.

[53] The financial sector was chosen due to the more recent surge in cyber-attacks on U.S. banks and citizens; the banking and finance sector also has the potential to suffer the most catastrophic damage to national security, U.S. economy, and lifestyle.

non-cooperation, perhaps even reluctance to cooperate, of both government agencies and privately owned businesses in charge of protecting our nation's CI.

D.   POTENTIAL EXPLANATIONS AND HYPOTHESES

Based on scholarly evidence presented in the literature review, there are three potential explanations for the failure of government and private sector cooperation in cybersecurity information-sharing. The author recognizes that, while the potential for other casual explanations or theories may exist, the three presented here are the most promising explanations to the complex question this thesis attempts to answer.

> Hypothesis One: Participation in PPPs is less likely to occur when either side fails to share cyber-related information in a timely and accurate manner.

> Hypothesis Two: Private companies feel threatened by cybersecurity regulations and standards that increase security costs, risk the loss of market share, and lack incentives, thus decreasing the likelihood of PPP participation.

> Hypothesis Three: Small-to-medium sized private sector companies lack the necessary resources to participate in information-sharing cybersecurity PPPs.

E.   METHODOLOGY

For the purpose of this research, Public-Private Partnerships (by definition provided earlier in the literature review) refers to both government and private sector entities that share in the resources, risks, and costs of delivering a service to the public.[54] Thus, the government-private associations explored in this research are synonymous with PPPs. Further discussion of PPPs is also provided in Chapter III. To help identify the barriers to establishing PPPs, this thesis examines cybersecurity information-sharing within the banking and finance CI sector. The three proposed hypotheses described above

---

[54] Cellucci, "Innovative Public-Private Partnerships," 4.

will be tested based on the evidence provided in Chapters III and IV in an attempt to answer the major research question of why information-sharing problems exist between government agencies and private companies.

For the purpose of this research, cyber-attacks involving major banks and corporations that affect the U.S. and world economy; personal identity theft that result in either potential or actual financial loss; and network breaches of major retail companies apply to the financial CI sector. While this thesis recognizes that other CI sectors share the same, if not more, dependency on cybersecurity alliances between government agencies and private sector companies, the finance sector has not only experienced a recent surge in cyber-attacks, but also have the potential to suffer the most catastrophic damage to our nation's security, economy, and way of life. Additionally, private-sector owners control the majority of CI systems within these sectors—further stressing the importance of evaluating the factors that both promote and challenge cybersecurity PPPs.

It is also important to note that while cyber-related incidents involving identity theft and breaches of major retail companies also fall under the IT sector, the majority of literature and evidence identifying the barriers to information-sharing between public and private entities is found within the banking and financial sector. However, in some instances, the lines between cybersecurity information sharing within some sectors can become blurred. For example, the FS and IT sectors; discussed in further detail in Chapter IV.

F.   OVERVIEW

Chapter II provides a background of recent cyber-attacks across the various sectors of CI to establish the importance and urgency of the topic. This chapter also provides a brief description of the most recent controversial cybersecurity policies and legislation applicable to this research. Chapter III identifies several factors that both promote and challenge the establishment of, and agency participation in, cybersecurity PPPs. Chapter IV assesses the current challenges facing the establishment of PPPs to advance cyber information sharing within the banking and finance CI sector. Chapter V provides a synopsis of the previous chapters, utilizes the case study findings to validate the three hypotheses, and offers recommendations for further research.

THIS PAGE INTENTIONALLY LEFT BLANK

II. BACKGROUND

A. RISE OF CYBER-RELATED THREATS

In a speech given at a cybersecurity conference in San Francisco, former FBI Director Robert Mueller said, "I am convinced that there are only two types of companies: those that have been hacked and those that will be," further adding, "they are even converging into one category: companies that have been hacked and will be hacked again."[55] Government agencies, businesses, and individuals alike have become more dependent on technology, and the desire and need for interconnectedness has led to increasing network vulnerability in both government and private sectors—including our nation's critical infrastructure.

Despite tireless efforts to secure government and commercial networks; increase critical infrastructure resiliency; and protect intellectual property, cyber-related attacks continue to increase across the globe. Today, no state can claim to be impermeable to cyber-related threats. The Center for Strategic and International Studies (CSIS) maintains an updated list of significant and successful cyber-attacks worldwide involving government agencies, the military, and the economy (where monetary loss exceeds one million dollars).[56] It is important to note that this list only contains what CSIS considers to be substantial and does not account for all cyber-attacks or attempts.

In the past decade, we have seen an increase of cyber-related attacks against U.S. networks and infrastructure. According to DHS, there were 50,000 cyber incidences reported between October 2011 and March 2012, which marked a historical increase in cyber-related attacks on multiple networks.[57] In fact, in 2012 alone, DHS recorded over

---

[55] Robert S. Mueller, "Remarks prepared for delivery," RSA Cyber Security Conference, Federal Bureau of Investigation, March 1, 2012, http://www.fbi.gov/news/speeches/combating-threats-in-the-cyber-world-outsmarting-terrorists-hackers-and-spies.

[56] CSIS, "Significant Cyber Events."

[57] Schmidt, "New Interest in Hacking."

198 attacks against the United States.[58] This sudden surge, coupled with a steady pattern of increasing vulnerability since 2010, created an overwhelming pressure on policymakers to pass legislation—granting the Department of Homeland Security (DHS) more oversight and regulation over the owners and operators of our Nation's Critical Infrastructure. The increasing trend of significant global cyber incidents over a 7-year span (2006–2013) is illustrated in Figure 1.

Photo Removed Due to Copyright Restrictions

Figure 1. Significant Cyber Incidents from 2006–2013[59]

From May 2006 to December 2013, according to CSIS, out of the 153 significant global cyber incidents (losses exceeding one million dollars), the United States alone experienced fifty-three—ranging from personal identity theft and cyber espionage, to the more recent Snowden leaks.[60] While some attacks have left behind minimal damage, other more sophisticated attacks have resulted in major security breaches—resulting in the loss of hundreds of millions of dollars.[61] The extent of damage caused by the Snowden leaks is still unknown.

---

[58] Tiffany Kaiser, "DHS: Cyber Attacks Against US Infrastructure Increased by 52 Percent in 2012," Daily Tech, January 10, 2013, http://www.dailytech.com/DHS+Cyber+Attacks+Against+US+Infrastructure+Increased+ by+52+Percent+in+2012/article29632.htm.

[59] Data retrieved from CSIS, "Significant Cyber Events."

[60] CSIS, "Significant Cyber Events."

[61] Ibid.

B.   POLICY AND LEGISLATION

Creating a policy on which everyone can agree is virtually impossible. In fact, in 1977, Congress introduced the Federal Computer Systems Protection Act, which attempted to establish penalties for computer crimes; unfortunately, the bill never passed. Throughout the next several years, federal agencies pressed policymakers to create laws against database breaches and a decade later, President Ronald Reagan signed the Computer Security Act of 1987, which intended to protect the databases of federal agencies against hacking. After the Morris worm attack of 1989 and continuous data theft in the early 1990s, it became obvious to policymakers that the Security Act of 1987 was failing.[62]

Throughout the 1990s, fears of the Y2K bug began to spread. As a result, the Clinton administration established a Presidential Commission of Critical Infrastructure Protection (PCCIP) in the summer of 1996 that aimed to protect vital systems against potential cyber disruptions, be they terrorism, espionage, or network hacking. As Y2K approached, policymakers spent tens of billions on protecting against the anticipated global cyber crash. When the arrival of Y2K passed uneventfully, critics began to question why the U.S. had bought into the Y2K hype while other countries had not.[63] Since 2000, the amount of cyber incidents and policy initiatives has increased substantially—gaining massive attention from both public and private sector stakeholders. This accumulation of cyber-attacks not only reinforced the necessity for increased government oversight and tougher policies aimed to harden cyber structures, it also signaled a worldwide caution to all nations to take a hard look at reforming cybersecurity policy.[64]

The United States has repeatedly struggled over the past several years to stay ahead of the opposition. In lieu of this battle, Congress and the president have passed,

---

[62] "Government and Cybersecurity," 1-2.

[63] Ibid.

[64] Andrea Peterson and Sean Pool, "Timeline: U.S. Security Policy in Context: A Look at President Obama's Latest Executive Order and the Policies that Preceded It," Science Progress, February 13, 2013, http://scienceprogress.org/2013/02/u-s-cybersecurity-policy-in-context/.

superseded, and abolished numerous cybersecurity policies; established U.S. Cyber Command (USCYBERCOM); formed the House Republican Cybersecurity Task Force; secretly released Presidential Policy Directive 20 (directive on cyber-attack defense); and released EO 13636 tasking NIST to develop a cybersecurity framework to assist owners and operators of CI to reduce cyber risks.[65] Today, cybersecurity policies and programs designed to protect our networks, databases, and critical infrastructure are numerous; and the road to get here has not been easy. Protecting our national security against evolving cyber-threats has been an overwhelming task requiring countless changes and updates to cybersecurity policy.

1.   CISPA and CISA

The most controversial bill on cybersecurity to date is the Cyber Intelligence Sharing and Protection Act (CISPA). In 2012, the House passed the bill despite heavy reproach from civil liberty organizations and critics who feared the bill would grant government and private agencies access to monitor individual online activity without oversight—so long as it was for cybersecurity purposes. CISPA came at a time when cyber-threats were on the rise and congress was receiving pressure from the financial sector and the White House to create legislation that encourages information sharing between government agencies and the private sector to prevent, mitigate, and respond to cyber-attacks. Supporters of the bill included tech companies IBM and Verizon; the financial institutions of Citibank and JPMorgan Chase; and the majority of House Republicans. Those opposed included the American Civil Liberties Union (ACLU); the Congressional Privacy Caucus; and President Barack Obama who felt the bill lacked confidentiality and regulation. Not surprisingly, the bill never made it past the Senate.[66] One year later, the bill resurfaced for a second round in Congress with the same results; however, this time the Senate refused to even vote, stating that the Senate Intelligence

---

[65] Peterson and Pool, "Timeline."

[66] Keith Wagstaff, "The Breakdown: Who Supports CISPA and Who Doesn't," *Time*, April 30, 2012, http://techland.time.com/2012/04/30/the-breakdown-who-supports-cispa-and-who-doesnt/.

Committee was currently working on a similar bill.[67] It was assumed that the next bill to replace the CISPA would be the NCCIP, until recently when Senators Dianne Feinstein (D-CA) and Saxby Chambliss (R-GA) revived a revised version of the CISPA bill for a third go-around. The new bill, the Cybersecurity Information Sharing Act of 2014 (CISA), calls upon NIST to establish the same standards and practices they have already done in Framework 1.0. To better distinguish CISA between the two previous bills that created much controversy over privacy and civil rights violations, drops the "P" (for Protection).[68] On April 18, 2014, CISA passed the House and, as the time of this research, was awaiting Senate approval.

2. NCCIP

With the recurring disappointment of CISPA over the past several years in Congress, Homeland Security Chair Michael McCaul (R-TX) and Bennie Thompson (D-MS) vowed to develop an information-sharing bill that allows DHS to assist the private sector, charged with protecting Critical Infrastructure, in combating cyber-threats. The National Cybersecurity and Critical Infrastructure Protection Act (NCCIP) of 2013, is not so much a Senate spinoff of CISPA as the current CISA bill, but rather the latest installment of information sharing legislation that amends the Homeland Security Act of 2002. Cybersecurity expert Tom Kellermann strongly supports the bill and is very optimistic that it will pass later this year. He has over 17 years of experience in cybersecurity risk response, and recently served on the Cybersecurity Mission for the 44th president.[69] In a recent interview, Kellermann stressed the bill's importance to the private sector and believed "it will act as a clearinghouse for cyber attacks and assistance," further adding, "Other countries have been providing this type of support, but

[67] Gerry Smith, "Senate Won't Vote on CISPA, Deals Blow Controversial Cyber Bill," *Huffington Post*, April 25, 2013, http://www.huffingtonpost.com/2013/04/25/cispa-cyber-bill_n_3158221.html.

[68] Zach Whittaker, "Failed Twice, Revived Again: CISPA Returns Despite Concerns Over Privacy, Data Sharing," ZDNet, April 30, 2014, http://www.zdnet.com/failed-twice-revived-again-cispa-returns-despite-concerns-over-privacy-data-sharing-7000028943/.

[69] Ashley Bennett, "Cybersecurity Expert Explains Importance of NCCIP Act," *Government Security News*, February 11, 2014, assessed on May 30, 2014, http://www.gsnmagazine.com/article/40197/cybersecurity_expert_explains_importance_nccip_act.

this would be a first in the U.S."[70] Working closely with DHS, representatives from the House Homeland Security Committee have been hard at work to finalize the bipartisan supported bill that could not come at a more crucial time when frequent and almost daily reported cyber-attacks occur across all sectors of critical infrastructure.[71]

3.   EO 13636

In February 2013, the White House released Executive Order 13636: Improving Critical Infrastructure Cybersecurity, due to the increasing potential of cyber-attacks that threaten our national security. The order establishes a standard for an information partnership between the private sector and government agencies on a voluntary basis. It calls on the Secretary of DHS, the director of DNI, the National Institute of Standards and Technology (NIST), and the Sector Specific Agencies (SSA), to establish a framework that improves resiliency and increases computer network security.[72] The main issue with this order was that participation in an information-sharing coalition by private companies was voluntary. Because of this, the debate between privacy and protection emerged, and many private firms seemed reluctant to share such information with government agencies. In hopes of encouraging private sector participation, the Secretary of DHS was ordered to establish an incentive program.[73]

4.   PPD-21

Released on the same day as EO 13636, the Presidential Policy Directive-21 was an overarching document addressing both physical and cyber threats against critical infrastructure; it replaced and updated the previous Homeland Security Presidential Directive-7 (HSPD-7). Similar to the requirements of EO 13636, the directive required the federal government to collaborate with state, local, tribal, and territorial agencies

---

[70] Bennett, "Cybersecurity Expert Explains."

[71] Nelson Peacock, "Cybersecurity Could be the Next Bipartisan Breakthrough," *The Hill*, January 22, 2014, assessed on May 30, 2014, http://thehill.com/blogs/congress-blog/technology/196026-cybersecurity-could-be-the-next-bipartisan-breakthrough.

[72] Executive Order no. 13636.

[73] Eric A. Fisher, et al., "The 2013 Cybersecurity Executive Order: Overview and Considerations for Congress," Congressional Research Service, March 1, 2013, 5–6, 9, http://www2.gwu.edu/~nsarchiv/NSAEBB/NSAEB B424/docs/Cyber-089.pdf.

(commonly referred to as SLTT), and the owners and operators in charge of critical infrastructure, to manage risks and increase resiliency against all hazards.[74] PPD-21 also established and identified 16 separate critical infrastructure sectors, including the financial services sector.[75] While EO 13636 focused exclusively on cyber-related threats by directing the Executive Branch to improve critical infrastructure cybersecurity, PPD-21 addressed all threats and hazards to critical infrastructure security and resilience, and called for an updated National Infrastructure Protection Plan (NIPP).[76] Despite its positive contributions in protecting national security, some have criticized PPD-21 for being too broad. Forbes contributor and author of *Surviving cyberwar*, Richard Stiennon, believed PPD-21 expects too much and sets unrealistic deadlines of government agencies and SSAs. He called PPD-21 his "worst nightmare," and a "top down solution that expresses the frustration of good intentions to 'do something.'"[77]

5.   NIPP

The National Infrastructure Protection Plan (NIPP) was an update to the previous NIPP as mandated by PPD-21. Drawing on lessons learned and experience gained since the previous NIPP, the new plan provided the framework for collective action across all CI sectors and all levels of government; incorporating both physical and cyber security elements, including the resilience of CI networks and assets, into one unity of effort aimed at increasing readiness and mitigating risk. The plan also established seven core tenants aimed to guide the entire CI community (national level down to the owner and operators) in the security planning process. Additionally, the NIPP introduced twelve *Calls to Action* intended to not only satisfy the goals of the plan, but to also guide all

---

[74] The White House, "Presidential Policy Directive/PPD-21: Critical Infrastructure Security and Resilience," U.S. General Services Administration, February 12, 2013, http://www.gsa.gov/portal/mediaId/176571/fileName/ATTCH_2_-_PPD-21.action.

[75] "Critical Infrastructure Sectors," Department of Homeland Security. accessed December, 15 2014, http://www.dhs.gov/critical-infrastructure-sectors.

[76] "Fact Sheet: Executive Order 13636 and Presidential Policy Directive (PPD)-21.

[77] Richard Stiennon, "PPD-21: Extreme Risk Management Gone Bad," *Forbes*, February 14, 2013, http://www.forbes.com/sites/richardstiennon/2013/02/14/ppd-21-extreme-risk-management-gone-bad/.

departments and agencies in a strategic direction to improve security and resilience of the nation's CI.[78]

C. NIST RESPONSE TO EO REQUIREMENT 7

After a year of hosting a series of workshops and revising multiple drafts, NIST released version 1.0 of its Cybersecurity Framework in February 2014. The framework was designed to be a cost-effective cyber-risk management tool allowing organizations to enhance critical infrastructure resiliency with minimal oversight from government agencies, and satisfied requirement seven of EO 13636.[79] The framework contains industry standards and best practices for managing cybersecurity risk, including procedures for protecting individual privacy and civil liberties during cybersecurity activities.[80] NIST's framework is not static; it is, however, a living and breathing risk management tool—shaped by both public and private sectors. Although originally intended for owners and operators of CI, the framework's application extends well beyond CI—aiding any corporation (large or small) in any industry, in identifying cyber-risks and strengthening networks. While critics downplay the framework for its flaws and omissions, government agencies and businesses—small and large—are beginning to find utility in the framework.

D. DHS RESPONSE TO EO REQUIREMENT 8

In February 2014, DHS launched C^3VP (commonly referred to as C-Cubed) to increase cybersecurity resiliency of critical infrastructure and to encourage use of the voluntary Framework. The C^3VP program was designed to assist SSAs in using and implementing the Cybersecurity Framework and satisfied requirement eight of EO 13636. The program is available in an unclassified, open-source forum that speaks to not only government and private agencies; it also offers academic, small business, and self-

---

[78] *National Infrastructure Protection Plan (NIPP 2013): Partnering to Enhance Protection and Resiliency*, U.S. Department of Homeland Security, (Washington, DC: 2009), http://www.dhs.gov/sites/default/files/publications/NIPP%202013_Partnering%20for%20Critical%20Infrastructure%20Security%20and%20Resilience_508_0.pdf.

[79] Jennifer Huergo, "NIST Releases Cybersecurity Framework Version 1.0," NIST, February 12, 2014, http://www.nist.gov/itl/csd/launch-cybersecurity-framework-021214.cfm.

[80] "Framework for Improving Critical Infrastructure Cybersecurity: Version 1.0."

service tools aimed at educating as many organizations and people as possible. Although the voluntary program is still in its early stages, the primary focus for this first phase is to provide guidance for those SSAs currently utilizing the Framework. In future phases, DHS plans to expand the scope of the program to sectors of critical infrastructure willing to adopt the Framework.[81] In a video teleconference at the Naval Postgraduate School in Monterey, CA, Director John F. Murphy, DHS Office of Cyber and Infrastructure Analysis (OCIA), felt the program has been "beneficial" and "a big step forward" in building relationships between the private sector and DHS.[82]

---

[81] "Critical Infrastructure Cyber Community Voluntary Program."

[82] Critical Infrastructure for Homeland Security (OS4621) course lecture with John F. Murphy at the Naval Postgraduate School, May 28, 2014.

THIS PAGE INTENTIONALLY LEFT BLANK

III. PUBLIC-PRIVATE PARTNERSHIPS IN CYBERSECURITY

A. INTRODUCTION

DHS describes public-private partnerships as conditions in which government agencies interact with private companies; these relationships are unique to other government-private associations as they both share in the resources, risks, and costs of delivering a service to the public.[83] The National Council for Public-Private Partnerships (NCPPP) defines public-private partnerships as:

> [A] contractual arrangement between a public agency (federal, state or local) and a private sector entity. Through this agreement, the skills and assets of each sector (public and private) are shared in delivering a service or facility for the use of the general public. In addition to the sharing of resources, each party shares in the risks and rewards potential in the delivery of the service and/or facility.[84]

As previously stated in the literature review, the concept of public-private partnerships is nothing new in the United States. PPPs can be traced back to the Colonial era in which the creation of a series of pharmaceutical laboratories led to government agencies utilizing private businesses to not only advance the progress of science but also benefit society.[85] In today's world of technology dependence and necessity for interconnectedness, many government and private sector entities believe that a cybersecurity information-sharing alliance between the government agencies and private businesses is the preeminent course of action to defend against cyber-related attacks. This chapter identifies and analyzes both factors that promote and challenge the establishment of information-sharing PPPs to defend against cyber-related threats. Identifying these factors not only provides the necessary evidence required to validate the three hypotheses proposed in Chapter I, but also helps identify why information-sharing barriers exist between government agencies and private companies.

---

[83] Cellucci, "Innovative Public-Private Partnerships," 4.

[84] The National Council for Public-Private Partnerships, "Seven Keys to Success: Public-Private Partnerships Defined, accessed January 3, 2015, http://www.ncppp.org/ppp-basics/7-keys/.

[85] Cellucci, "Innovative Public-Private Partnerships," 4.

B.   FACTORS PROMOTING PPPS

In 2002, the California Management Review featured an article that called into question management's role in cybersecurity. While the authors argue that no organization can claim to enjoy perfect security, they do offer a few guidelines for those in the executive level of companies for consideration in minimizing risk while implementing a well-balanced and organized plan to combat cyber-threats. Despite being over a decade old, these findings still set a precedent that scholars and cyber experts have been stressing the importance of PPPs as both a tool and strategy to help combat cybersecurity issues between the public and private sector long before the recent surge of cyber-attacks.[86] Although the report's focus was mainly on management's role in encouraging PPP participation to enhance cybersecurity, several benefits for utilizing PPPs aimed at securing vital networks of CI were identified. Certain costs are reduced when private companies express their views on the economic consequences of poor information security and when they agree to share their solutions to common security problems with government agencies. This not only establishes a reputation between private companies and government clients, it also improves private-government relations and allows both sides the opportunity to gain a better understanding of each other's priorities and goals. Furthermore, participation in PPPs allows managers the opportunity to implement shared best practices and, more importantly, a voice in shaping policy in areas, such as the Freedom of Information Act (FOIA) and anti-trust laws—policies that play a major role in public-private sector relations.[87]

Globalization and a rise in privatization of the public sector have resulted in many private companies assuming responsibility of Critical Infrastructure Protection (CIP). This has created a challenge for both public and private sectors as government and private markets alone have become increasingly incapable of keeping up with cyber

---

[86] Amitava Dutta and McCrohan, Kevin, "Management's Role in Information Security in a Cyber Economy," *California Management Review* 45, no. 1 (Fall, 2002): 67–87, http://search.proquest.com/docview/215864793?accountid=12702.

[87] Ibid., 76.

threats and providing security for the majority of CI sectors.[88] According to Myriam Dunn Cavelty and Manuel Suter, Center for Security Studies (CSS) in Zurich, Switzerland, cooperation between public and private entities in charge of CIP is essential. Cavelty adds that PPPs "have become the preferred solution in the field of CIP."[89] They give a lot of credit to the formation of sector-specific ISACs within the United States—an answer to Clinton's Presidential Decision Directive (PDD) 63. Although much work still lies ahead in improving how ISACs work horizontally (with other ISACs), the authors note that since 1999—the creation of the Financial Services ISAC (FS-ISAC)—ISACs have been performing as successful examples of cybersecurity information-sharing PPPs. Furthermore, many foreign governments have also seen success in creating similar PPPs that enjoy information-sharing between government and private industry designed to protect CI.[90] Further discussion of the FS-ISAC, including its contribution to cybersecurity information sharing, is found in Chapter IV. While Cavelty and Suter reiterate the utility and necessity of information-sharing PPPs outlined in President Bill Clinton's Commission on Critical Infrastructure Protection (PCCIP)—which, among other tasks, called for the integration of private owners and operators of CI to help shape security policy—the majority of their work is based on identifying limitations to PPPs of CIP; therefore, those findings are discussed in the next section (Challenges and Limitations).[91]

Although this research focuses on information-sharing alliances that help protect CI from cyber threats, it is important to recognize the utility of PPPs in increasing resilience during and after natural or manmade disasters—regardless of whether those disasters or events involve the use of cyber. Several benefits of PPPs formed to protect CI during times of disaster and recovery can be valuable in combating other types of threats, such as cyber-attacks. A study in 2009, conducted by the National Incident Management

---

[88] Myriam Dunn Cavelty and Suter, Manuel, "Public-Private Partnerships are no Silver Bullet: An Expanded Governance model for Critical Infrastructure Protection," *International Journal of Critical Infrastructure Protection* Vol. 4, no. 2 (March, 2009): 179, doi:10.1016/j.ijep.2009.08.006.

[89] Ibid., 180.

[90] Ibid., 181.

[91] Ibid.

Systems and Advanced Technologies Institute, identified several benefits and challenges in using PPPs to enhance resiliency during post-disaster response and recovery. The authors examine how resilience and PPPs can align to enhance disaster recovery and, in turn, recommend a framework that incorporates mutually supporting entities, such as PPPs, local communities, and critical infrastructure key resources (CI/KR).[92] The study found that PPPs create unique opportunities to increase resilience during the response and recovery phases by enabling decision makers the ability to identify and focus the capabilities of both public and private entities where they are best needed.[93] Other benefits include reducing certain limitations, such as trust, commonly associated with public-private collaboration by establishing guidelines that increase transparency and ensure accountability across the board.[94] Trust between government and private firms wishing to share information about cyber threats have become a major and more recent concern. When stressful events occur, such as major disaster or cyber-attacks, trust between both public and private sectors is paramount.

The most prominent benefits of establishing PPPs can be found in a report published by DHS in the summer of 2010. The report identified three major benefits in utilizing PPPs in general: First, PPPs increase efficiency in completing tasks and requirements; second, they significantly reduce taxpayer spending; third, they improve regulation compliance and increase service quality.[95] DHS Chief Commercialization Officer Tom Cellucci believes that the PPP model is being used to "make positive changes in the way government and industry can work together" in solving homeland security needs.[96] While the report does not focus on cybersecurity specifically and bases its findings primarily from commercialized-based PPPs, it does produce several worthwhile benefits for policymakers to consider in fostering PPPs for cybersecurity

---

[92] Geoffrey T. Stewart, Kolluru, Ramesh, and Smith, Mark, "Leveraging Public-Private Partnerships to Improve Community Resilience in Times of Disaster," *International Journal of Physical Distribution & Logistics Management* 39, no. 5 (2009): 345, http://search.proquest.com/docview/232592275?accountid=12702.

[93] Ibid., 344.

[94] Ibid., 346.

[95] Cellucci, "Innovative Public-Private Partnerships," 4.

[96] Ibid., 2.

information-sharing. Citizens (or taxpayers) benefit from better protection and less taxation; government agencies develop a better understanding of private sector needs and use less public resources; and private companies become better positioned to support public interests with its capabilities, ultimately contributing to the nation's security. DHS contends that PPPs produce a *win-win-win* scenario for all parties involved.[97] Former DHS Secretary Michael Chertoff also believes that PPPs are a better fit than simply allowing the government to prescribe cybersecurity policy to private companies. Chertoff believes that employing PPPs in cybersecurity would allow information to flow in both directions with the government offering research and intelligence, while the private sector reciprocating with educating government agencies on data mining and analysis it collects.[98]

Neustar—a private corporation that analyzes real-time data within the Internet and telecommunications industries—praised the U.S. government's effort in facilitating the establishment of PPPs to meet the nation's challenges in cybersecurity. At a recent forum hosted by the Bipartisan Policy Center (BPC), Neustar's Chief Technology Officer Mark Bregman commended the government's efforts to bring both public and private sectors together to meet cybersecurity challenges to the nation's economy and national security. Neustar is a member of the Executive Branch's National Security Telecommunications Advisory Committee (NSTAC) and the Federal Communications Commission's (FCC) Communications, Security, Reliability and Interoperability Council (CSRIC)—PPPs that work together to address cyber threats.[99]

C.   CHALLENGES AND LIMITATIONS

While factors that promote the use of PPPs in cybersecurity are numerous, there are also several challenges and limitations to establishing and employing them to effectively counter cyber threats. Referring back to the findings in the 2002 California

---

[97] Cellucci, "Innovative Public-Private Partnerships," 16, 41.

[98] John Curran, "Chertoff: Cybersecurity Requires More Public-Private Cooperation," *Cybersecurity Policy Report* (May 02, 2011): 1, http://search.proquest.com/docview/867525563?Accountid=12702.

[99] "Neustar Commends the U.S. Government for Encouraging Public-Private Partnerships to Meet Cyber Security Challenges," *Business Wire,* Feb 22, 2012, http://search.proquest.com/docview/922610532?accountid=12702.

Management Review that focused on management's role in cybersecurity, the authors discuss the existence of hardships in forming PPPs—even over a decade ago. Despite the benefits realized from information-sharing PPPs, collaboration between two divergent sectors is neither an easy task—nor does it occur automatically.[100] Perhaps the primary concern for stakeholders on both sides has been the ability to achieve and maintain trust between private sector companies and their government counterparts. Beyond the obstacle of attaining trust lies cooperation between both parties, which requires not only support from an appropriate number of personnel to satisfy requirements but also an adequate amount of funding and resources to accomplish agreed upon objectives—the latter being the most difficult to achieve due to shortages felt on both sides. Furthermore, information-sharing PPPs need proficient leaders capable of fusing the divergent and sometimes conflicting interests and cultures of both government agencies and private companies.[101] The report also lists FOIA as another prohibiting factor to information-sharing between the government and the private sector; however, since 2002 there have been several bills awaiting congressional approval that allegedly address the legal issues of private sector companies sharing information about cyber threats to the government. In his statement before the Committee on the Judiciary Senate, former Assistant Secretary for Policy for DHS, Paul Rosenzweig, stated that the proposed exemptions to the FOIA were "both wise and essential," further expressing that "Current law[s] are, at best, ambiguous (and at worst prohibitory) and therefore impedes [sic] the creating and sharing of cyber threat and vulnerability information."[102] He, among others, believes that legal barriers to cybersecurity information-sharing PPPs are a primary concern of the majority of private-sector stakeholders.

Myriam Dunn Cavelty and Manuel Suter's extensive work in cybersecurity CIP also revealed several limitations in establishing and maintaining PPPs aimed at protecting

---

[100] Dutta and McCrohan, "Management's Role," 75–76.

[101] Ibid.

[102] Paul Rosenzweig, "Cybersecurity Information Sharing and the Freedom of Information Act: Statement before the Committee on the Judiciary United States Senate," The Heritage Foundation, March 14, 2012, http://www.heritage.org/research/testimony/2012/03/cybersecurity-information-sharing-and-the-freedom-of-information-act.

CI.[103] First, they argue that the traditional PPP term is not applicable in the field of CIP since the majority of existing PPPs are project-based (designed to create efficiency) rather than time-based (aimed at building trust). Information-sharing between two diverse entities can only occur when mutual trust has been established, which requires a significant amount of time. Understanding this distinction, according to Cavelty and Suter, is necessary when thinking about PPPs in the field of CIP.[104] Second, while the private sector owns and operates the majority of the nation's CI, it is also increasingly finding itself in charge of protecting it. Since the fundamental duty of the state is protection of its citizens, delegating the task of security to the private sector raises some concerns over converging interests. While both public and private sectors share in the concern of disclosing information—government fears of unauthorized recipients gaining access to sensitive information and private sector fears of government security leaks— their interests begin to diverge with the private sector becoming more concerned about business continuity than resolving state concerns over security issues. Furthermore, because the majority of private companies conduct their business abroad, they can only moderately enjoy the benefits of national collaboration.[105] Third, and probably the biggest challenge to PPPs, is that most successful information-sharing exchanges occur inside much smaller circles, in which public and private agencies already enjoy some familiarity and degree of trust from previous relations. The underlying issue of information-sharing between public and private businesses is that in order to achieve trust, one needs collaboration; however, the success of that relationship relies heavily on trust. This is what the authors refer to as, the "classic assurance problem" or "'chicken-and-egg' paradox."[106] Cavelty and Suter argue that forming new PPPs that share sensitive information is more difficult because it requires a high demand of mutual trust and are most likely doomed to fail in larger frameworks.[107]

---

[103] Cavelty and Suter, "Public-Private Partnerships," 181.

[104] Ibid.

[105] Ibid.

[106] Ibid., 182.

[107] Ibid.

In 2011, former DHS Deputy Secretary William Lynn III also believed that trust issues; legislation preventing information exchange; fear of client and stakeholder criticism; and inter-government agency conflicts were some of the top challenges facing the public-private sector collaboration in the cyber domain.[108] A major limitation to information-sharing PPPs, such as ISACs, is that most are voluntary in nature; in other words, they can only share information they receive. While the U.S. government facilitates the organization of ISACs to collect, analyze, and disseminate cyber threat information, problems such as free-riding often result from inadequate incentives. Furthermore, not all ISACs share information with other ISACs, which greatly limits the distribution of critical threat information to other industries; thus, leaving ISAC databases unreliable and resulting in analysts producing incomplete results.[109]

Manuel Suter, who is also affiliated with the International Cyber Center at George Mason University, held a cybersecurity workshop in Zurich, Switzerland, in the summer of 2010 where he discussed some of the challenges and best practices of cybersecurity PPPs aimed at protecting CI, and how to best manage those partnerships. Some of the major challenges facing cyber PPPs identified include:

- Unclear delineation of roles and responsibilities

- Lack of trust between partners

- Diverging interests

- Misplaced expectations[110]

Suter also found that some private companies that become frustrated and have backed out of partnerships due specifically to the unwillingness of government actors to

---

[108] Erik Bataller, "Cyber Partnerships," *InformationWeek* no. 1295 (Mar 28, 2011): 22, http://search.proquest.com/docview/860133412?accountid=12702.

[109] Julie McNally, "Improving Public-Private Sector Cooperation on Cyber Event Reporting," Academic Conferences International Limited, 2013, 151–2, http://search.proquest.com/docview/1549246645?accountid=12702.

[110] Manuel Suter, "Unpacking Public-Private Partnerships: Identifying Differences, Challenges and Practices of Collaboration in Cyber Security," George Mason University International Cyber Center, accessed January 10, 2015, http://www.internationalcybercenter.org/workshops/cs-ga-2010–1/cs-ga-2010/msuter.

reasonably cooperate. He concluded that while PPPs are vital in satisfying cybersecurity policies, they are difficult to establish.[111] His findings echo a lot of the same major challenges to PPPs that have been highlighted throughout this chapter.

D. CYBERSECURITY PPPS IN ACTION

Perhaps the best approach for analyzing the effectiveness of PPPs is to examine a few, already-established, partnerships between the government and private business aimed at combating cyber-attacks and threats. As a result of the military's overwhelming task of protecting cyberspace against intrusion, U.S. Cyber Command (USCYBERCOM) was created in the summer of 2009 and became fully operational in late 2010. The consolidation comprised of the four service entities in charge of cyberwarfare (U.S. Army, Navy, Air Force, and Marine Corps) and is headed by one appointed service commander, Admiral Michael S. Rogers (at the time of this study).[112] One of USCYBERCOMs missions is to partner with various government and non-government entities aimed at combating cyber threats, according to Deputy Defense Secretary William J. Lynn III.[113] In 2010, as a part of the Pentagon's Cyberstrategy, Lynn stressed the importance of USCYBERCOMs partnership with DHS and private enterprise in exchanging cyber-related threat information and managing mutual vulnerabilities. "The effort to defend the United States will only succeed if it is coordinated across the government, with allies, and with partners in the commercial sector," argued Lynn.[114]

Another PPP of interest is Enduring Security Framework—the collaboration of several major IT and defense companies, along with representatives from DHS, ODNI (Office of the Director of National Intelligence), and DOD—was launched toward the end of 2008.[115] Top executives from the private sector are granted a one-day top secret

---

[111] Suter, "Unpacking Public-Private Partnerships."

[112] "U.S. Cyber Command Fact Sheet," U.S. Strategic Command, accessed January 8, 2015, http://www.stratcom.mil/factsheets/2/Cyber_Command/.

[113] William J. Lynn III, "Defending a New Domain: The Pentagon's Cyberstrategy." *Foreign Affairs* 89, no. 5 (September 2010): 102, http://search.proquest.com/docview/815278494?accountid=12702.

[114] Ibid., 102–3.

[115] Ibid., 105.

clearance and meet in Washington, DC, two to three times a year to discuss current cyber threats, capabilities, cyber weapons, and share in cybersecurity best practices. CEOs are then able to take this information back to their respective companies to protect their own networks against the latest cyber-attacks.[116] The most recent meeting, held on September 14, 2014, included a discussion on insider threats, DDoS, and destructive malware.[117] At the time of his report, Lynn stressed the need for other agencies, such as The National Security Agency (NSA), to utilize their capabilities outside the government domain (.gov) to defend against critical network intrusions and cyber-attacks in commercialized domains (.com). "The best-laid plans for defending military networks will matter little if civilian infrastructure… is not secure," argued Lynn.[118]

The National Cybersecurity and Communications Integration Center (NCCIC) is another public sector effort to encourage and establish cybersecurity PPPs. The NCCIC works with 18 separate private-sector industries to maintain an open dialog about cybersecurity threats and offers assistance when necessary; Facebook and Twitter were two recent examples.[119] Homeland Security's National Cyber Security Division (NCSD) has also worked with private groups to investigate cyber-attacks, such as the Stuxnet worm—which infected several critical networks in the countries of Iran and Indonesia— and has facilitated cyber exercises, such as Cyber Storm III.[120] More recent examples of private firms working with federal agencies to combat cyber incidents include Microsoft and a government CERT team—whose joint efforts were responsible for dismantling the Waledec botnet (a virus that infected Windows users worldwide); the NSA also assisted Google with an investigation into the Internet giant's security breach.[121] These are just a

---

[116] Tom Gjelton, "Cyber Briefings 'Scare the Bejeezus' Out of CEOs," NPR web, May 9, 2012, http://www.npr.org/2012/05/09/152296621/cyber-briefings-scare-the-bejeezus-out-of-ceos.

[117] Critical Infrastructure Partnership Advisory Council (CIPAC), "Cross Sector Enduring Security Framework (ESF) Operations Working Group Agenda," Department of Homeland Security, accessed January, 15 2015, http://www.dhs.gov/sites/default/files/publications/cipac-cs-esf-ops-agenda-09–17–14–508_0.pdf.

[118] Lynn, "Defending a New Domain," 104.

[119] Bataller, "Cyber Partnerships," 22.

[120] Ibid., 23.

[121] Ibid.

few cases that not only illustrate the advantages of public-private collaboration, but also promote the use of PPPs in strengthening cybersecurity efforts.

Between 2008 and 2011, the information-sharing efforts of the National Cyber Forensics and Training Alliance (NCFTA) resulted in hundreds of criminal investigations and prosecutions in cyber-related crimes.[122] NCFTA—a non-profit corporation—is the only international cross-sector PPP model that unites over 500 subject matter experts (SME) from both public and private sectors worldwide; consisting of members from the FBI, U.S. Immigration and Customs Enforcement (ICE), and Postal Inspection Service that collaborate with private industry, academia, and law enforcement to thwart cyber-attacks and threats. Since its inception in 2002, the coalition's focus has been to support the timely exchange of the most up-to-date cyber threats, including cyber-related crimes that occur within the IT and finance sectors, among others.[123]

A more recent and successful PPP model comes from the development of NIST's Cybersecurity Framework 1.0 (discussed in Chapter II). After a year of hosting a series of workshops and revising multiple drafts, NIST released version 1.0 of the framework—a structured roadmap designed to improve resiliency, increase computer network security, and encourage companies to discuss and evaluate best practices for managing cybersecurity risk.[124] While the framework was initiated by the White House, it is far from any government-regulated standard. NIST "went to great lengths to collect, distill, and incorporate feedback from security professionals," said Wyatt Kash of *InformationWeek*.[125] He praised NIST for its public-private methodology of employing both public and private sector stakeholders into a PPP to develop the framework. "The framework has cred, as its recommendations come not from Washington regulators, but

---

[122] Ron Plesco and Phyllis Schneck, "Criminal Public-Private Partnerships: Why can't we do that?" Georgetown Journal of International Affairs (Fall, 2011): 153, http://search.proquest.com/docview/911784343?accountid=12702.

[123] Ibid.

[124] Executive Order no. 13636.

[125] Wyatt Kash, "Why Businesses Can't Ignore US Cybersecurity Framework," February 14, 2014, http://www.informationweek.com/government/cybersecurity/why-businesses-cant-ignore-us-cybersecurity-framework/d/d-id/1113838.

from industry experts who've combatted cyberattacks," added Kash.[126] NIST executives state that their intention is to preserve the framework as a "living document," and expects to receive continual updates and improvements "as industry provides feedback on implementation;" further claiming that "lessons learned will be integrated into future versions." [127] From April 2013 to April 2014, NIST hosted five Framework Workshops and its first Private Engineering workshop to discuss development, solicit questions, and request feedback from industry, cybersecurity experts, and government agencies.[128] NIST recently conducted its second Privacy Engineering workshop in September 2014 and its sixth Framework Workshop in October—its first gathering of industry stakeholders, academia, and the government since the framework's debut. Stakeholders from both sides assessed industry use and awareness of the framework and addressed issues identified from industry feedback.[129] NIST has been very aggressive in making steady improvements to the framework to ensure companies can adapt to evolving cyber threats; private sector owners and operators of CI—the framework's end-users—have been the key component in providing recommendations to shape the framework. IBM Security Advisor, Diana Kelley, believes the "Framework can bring valuable guidance to all industries and organizations that depend on IT for their operations because it brings a common language and model to the process of managing cybersecurity risk."[130] Despite the framework's infancy, it has made headlines. In the recent Heartbleed Saga—a newly discovered vulnerability in OpenSSL (Secure Socket layer) encryption software—government agencies utilized the framework throughout the entire process from

---

[126] Kash, "Why Businesses Can't Ignore..."

[127] National Institute of Standards and Technology, "NIST Roadmap for Improving Critical Infrastructure Cybersecurity," U.S. Department of Commerce, February 12, 2014, 1, http://www.nist.gov/cyberframework/upload/ roadmap-021214.pdf.

[128] National Institute of Standards and Technology, "Cybersecurity Framework–Workshops and Events," U.S. Department of Commerce, last updated September 12, 2014, http://www.nist.gov/ cyberframework /cybersecurity-framework-events.cfm.

[129] National Institute of Standards and Technology, "6th Cybersecurity Framework Workshop," U.S. Department of Commerce, last updated September 12, 2014, http://www.nist.gov/cyberframework/6th-cybersecurity-framework-workshop-october-29–30–2014.cfm.

[130] Diana Kelley, "Application Security Risk Management and the NIST Cybersecurity Framework," March 3, 2014, http://securityintelligence.com/nist-cybersecurity-framework-application-security-risk-management/#.VBSx1xLn_IV.

identifying the threat to recovery.[131] While private industry and government agencies seemed to lack common syntax, risk-management, and structure in cybersecurity, NISTs Framework seems to be filling that void and adding to the growing list of successful PPPs in cybersecurity.

E.   SUMMARY

As economies, government agencies, businesses, and individuals continue to depend on the advances of technology for everything from banking and trading to communicating and shopping, cyber-attacks to U.S. critical infrastructure and national security are becoming more sophisticated and harder to defend. Unfortunately, this desire and need for interconnectedness has led to an increasing vulnerability in both government and private sectors. This chapter analyzed factors that promote and challenge the establishment of information-sharing PPPs to help defend against cyber-related threats. It also discussed current cybersecurity PPPs in action—such as Enduring Security Framework, the NCFTA, and the development of NIST's Cybersecurity Framework 1.0. While the utility of PPPs in cybersecurity is steadily increasing, several challenges still remain. Three common barriers are lack of trust; legal concerns protecting private companies from litigation; and diverging interests and missed expectations between government and private companies. The conclusion of this chapter leads us to the major thesis question: if there are so many successful cases and incentives in utilizing PPPs to increase security and efficiency in both public and private sectors, then why is there an apparent failure of government and private sector cooperation in cybersecurity information-sharing? The following case study will address this problem by identifying the current issues surrounding this dilemma within the banking and finance CI sector.

---

[131] Nicole Blake Johnson, "The Cybersecurity Framework's Role in the Heartbleed Saga," *Fedtechmagazine,* July 3, 2014, http://www.fedtechmagazine.com/article/2014/07/cybersecurity-frameworks-role-heartbleed-saga.

THIS PAGE INTENTIONALLY LEFT BLANK

IV. CASE STUDY: INFORMATION SHARING WITHIN THE BANKING AND FINANCE SECTOR

A. INTRODUCTION

This chapter assesses the current challenges facing the establishment of PPPs to advance cyber information sharing within the banking and finance sector of U.S. Critical Infrastructure. For the purpose of this research (as mentioned earlier in Chapter I), the cyber-related attacks examined in this thesis are those involving major banks and corporations that affect the U.S. and world economy; personal identity theft that results in either potential or actual financial loss; and network breaches of major retail companies apply to the financial CI sector. While cyber-related incidents involving identity theft and breaches of major retail companies also fall under the IT sector, this thesis found that the majority of literature and evidence identifying the barriers to information-sharing between public and private entities exists within the banking and financial sector.

To establish the necessity for both public and private sector collaboration in cybersecurity, this chapter first offers a brief background of the most prominent cyber-attacks that have affected the finance sector—including threats originating from China and Iran, and the recent surge in identity theft—to help establish the urgency of why both public and private agencies need to establish cybersecurity information-sharing partnerships. Second, it offers a brief overview of the FS-ISAC and its contribution to cybersecurity information-sharing between the public and sector. Finally, this chapter identifies the more recent barriers to public-private cooperation in cybersecurity to help validate the three hypotheses introduced in Chapter I. These three explanations are validated in the final chapter.

B. BACKGROUND

In the summer of 2012, the Director of the National Security Agency (NSA), General Keith Alexander, announced that cyber-attacks on U.S. critical infrastructure companies had increased seventeen times between 2009 and 2011. He argued that attacks on our nation's critical infrastructure are far more damaging than espionage and other similar computer crimes. "On a scale of 1 to 10," according to Alexander, "American preparedness for a large-scale cyber-attack is around a 3."[132] At the time of his statement, Congress was in the process of passing legislation that authorizes government agencies to intervene in defending the networks of the private companies that operate our nation's infrastructure.[133]

By ignoring multiple DDoS attacks on local websites only weeks prior to the Russian troop movement into South Ossetia in August 2008, the Georgian government allowed its cyber infrastructure to be shut down.[134] Although forbidden by the Hague (V) Conventions of 1907, the Georgian government set up a temporary cyber-shop in three other countries, including the United States, in order to counter the Russian attack and protect its cyber infrastructure.[135] U.S.-based servers, operated by TS Host, a multi-million dollar company that provides secure servers for businesses, provided a safe location for the Georgian government to re-launch its more critical websites; however, neither TS Host nor the Georgian government received permission to do so.[136] While the United States has authority under the Hague (V) Conventions of 1907 to remain neutral[137] during a cyber-war carried out between two other combatant nations, this incident revealed that governments have minimal oversight on countries like Georgia that seek out private companies, seeded in U.S. territory, to render aid during a crisis like the Russian-Georgia War.[138] Although these cyber-attacks were specifically concentrated on Georgia's government and economy, it validated not only Russia's capability to conduct

---

[132] David E. Sanger and Schmitt, Eric, "Rise is Seen in Cyberattacks Targeting US Infrastructure," *New York Times*, July 26, 2012, http://www.nytimes.com/2012/07/27/us/cyberattacks-are-up-national-security-chief-says.html?_r=0.

[133] Michael McCaul, "Hardening Our Defenses Against Cyberwarfare," *The Wall Street Journal*, March 5, 2013, http://online.wsj.com/news/articles/SB10001424127887324662404578336862508763 442.

[134] Stephen W. Korns and Joshua E. Kastenberg, "Georgia's Cyber Left Hook," *Parameters* 38, no. 4 (2009): 60. Proquest Research Library (198032208).

[135] Ibid., 62.

[136] Ibid., 67.

[137] For further information on cyber neutrality see, Michael N Schmitt, Tallinn Manual On the International Law *Applicable to Cyber Warfare: Prepared By the International Group of Experts At the Invitation of the NATO Cooperative* Cyber Defence Centre of Excellence (New York: Cambridge University Press, 2013): 248-255.

[138] Korns and Kastenberg, "Georgia's Cyber Left Hook,".61-2.

such attacks, but alsoits will to utilize cyber warfare offensively. Today, policymakers face the challenge of preventing a repeat like Georgia's demonstration of exploiting U.S. cyber assets to remain active during war, or much worse, directly attack U.S. banking and finance CI. The majority of cyber-related attacks on U.S. banking and finance have originated in the countries of China and Iran. For this reason, it is helpful to identify and discuss these occurrences below separately. Additionally, attacks involving identity theft and the 2014 surge in criminal cyber activity are also discussed.

1.   China

In January 2010, a group of hackers from China infiltrated Morgan Stanley's computer network, although no reports indicate the extent of damage caused by the network breach. Morgan Stanley's cyber security firm was responsible for leaking the incident to the public. From March 2010 until April 2011, twenty separate illegal wire transfers occurred between several U.S. businesses and Chinese trade companies due to the compromise of online banking credentials. According to the FBI, the fraudulent transactions cost an estimated $11 million in individual losses—totaling $20 million overall. During a six-month network breach that began in October 2011, a hacker from China targeted the intellectual property of 48 chemical and defense companies, according to the virus-smashing firm Symantec. In December 2011, hackers from China penetrated the U.S. Chamber of Commerce networks, which contained several communications on trade policy secrets between U.S. companies. Several media outlets linked the People's Liberation Army (PLA) to the breach. News syndicates: *The New York Times, Wall Street Journal, Washington Post,* and *Bloomberg News* also attributed China to several cyber-attacks in January 2013. What was most potentially damaging, although not specific to the finance and IT sectors, was the breach of the U.S. Army Corps of Engineers' network in May 2013, in which Chinese hackers gained direct access to the inventory and data of all U.S. dams.[139]

---

[139] CSIS, "Significant Cyber Events."

2.   Iran

Iran has also had its fair share of credit for cyber-attacks on the U.S. financial infrastructure. The most attributable Iranian-linked hacker group to date has been the Izzad-Din al-Qassam Cyber Fighters, which is also known for its ties to the terrorist group Hamas. The cyber-attacks from the group span between September 2012 and June 2013. The most noteworthy of attacks began with the group's launch of *Operation Ababil*, which involved a series of continuous Distributed Denial of Service (DDoS) attacks aimed at the websites of several U.S. financial institutions in September 2012. One month later, reports indicated that six major U.S. banks fell victim to DDoS attacks. In January 2013, the group once again claimed ownership of similar DDoS attacks on the iconic financial institution, U.S. Bank. From March to June 2013, the group continued to target reputable U.S. financial institutions under *Operation Ababil*. During its twenty-one month cyber-wrath, the Cyber Fighters conducted three phases of DDoS attacks. Toward the close of the third phase, the group warned of a fourth; however, since that announcement, the group has been unnervingly silent.[140] This has likely contributed to increased security measures taken by major U.S. financial institutions immediately following the group's announcement.[141] Despite the ominous silence from the Izzad-Din al-Qassam Cyber Fighters, other anonymous Iranian hackers have emerged, amassing their efforts to attack the wide spectrum of U.S. critical infrastructure.[142]

3.   Identity Theft

Identity theft is a major and more recent area of concern in the cyber world. Gone are the days when simply covering up an ATM pin number, shredding bank statements, or even encrypting the network is adequate or acceptable. Criminals today are more sophisticated and efficient—using the very same technology we use and enjoy against us

---

[140] Tracey Kitten, "DDoS: Attackers Announce Phase 4," Bank Info Security, Information Security Media Group, July 23, 2013, http://www.bankinfosecurity.com/ddos-attackers-announce-phase-4-a-5929/op-1.

[141] Matt Egan, "Banks Deploy Shields to Block New Wave of Cyber Attacks," Fox Business, July 31, 2013, http://www.foxbusiness.com/technology/2013/07/31/banks-deploy-shields-to-block-new-wave-cyber-attacks/.

[142] CSIS, "Significant Cyber Events."

to steal our identities and livelihood without ever knowing us or even leaving their living rooms. One cybercriminal that stands out is Albert Gonzalez who, up until the more recent Target and Sony hacks, pulled off the largest case of identity theft in U.S. history. Between 2006 and 2008, Gonzalez and a few Russian associates allegedly hacked over 130 million credit card accounts via the websites of five major retailers. [143]

In December 2009, a group of hackers from China infiltrated the networks of search engine mogul Google, as well as the networks of some 30 other companies. According to Google, the hackers were successful in collecting valuable data, including gaining access to Google's password management system and user e-mail accounts. Another noteworthy case involving the tech giant Google occurred in April 2011, in which Google announced that the Gmail account passwords of hundreds of distinguished individuals had been compromised by hackers in China using phishing scams. The following month, hackers infiltrated the popular Sony PlayStation network and stole the personal information of over 80 million clients—the breach cost Sony over $170 million—although this incident has been overshadowed by the more recent Sony computer system breach and shutdown in late 2014.[144]

Similar to the actions of Albert Gonzalez a few years earlier, a group of hackers in June 2011 managed to acquire the data from 360,000 Citibank credit card owners. Two years later, the FBI charged five Ukrainian and Russian hackers with possession of over 160 million credit card numbers, resulting in a loss of over a hundred million dollars. More recently, in December 2013, credit and debit card information of over 40 million shoppers at the retail giant Target were stolen and sold on a well-known organized crime forum in Eastern Europe.[145] The full magnitude of this breach was still under investigation at the time of this research.

Recent high-profile cyber events, such as Heartbleed, Target's data breach, and Sony Corp's hack, among several others, have led to new talks within other CI sectors,

---

[143] Aly Weisman, "A Timeline of the Crazy Events in the Sony Hacking Scandal," *Business Insider,* December 9, 2014, http://www.businessinsider.com/sony-cyber-hack-timeline-2014-12.

[144] Ibid.

[145] CSIS, "Significant Cyber Events."

including the Information Technology (IT), and Communications Sectors. The Federal Communications Commission (FCC) recently began an initiative to align its cybersecurity activities with NIST's Framework—calling on all members within the industry to invest in innovation and professional development. FCC Chairman Tom Wheeler stated that the private sector will lead the initiative, but be government backed, and will "identify public goals, work with the affected stakeholders… and let that experience inform whether there is any need for next steps."[146] Wheeler believes that aligning efforts with the framework will increase situational awareness, minimize cybersecurity risk, and improve innovation and professional development within the technology and communications industry.[147] Increasing attacks on critical networks that hold personal data stresses the need for a more structured approach involving both public and private sector collaboration.

4. 2014 Surge in Cyber Criminal Activity

While the previous section focused on cybersecurity issues between the years 2006 and 2013, the recent surge of cyber-attacks on networks that hold personal data in 2014 (during the writing of this thesis) cannot be overlooked; thus, they are noted herein to help establish the importance of this research. A recent article published by *Forbes* listed the top 20 major data breaches of 2014 from malware designed to seize debit and credit card information to the compromise of private records, including social security numbers.[148] Table 1 lists the top ten breaches based on the highest number of people affected and the most potentially damaging.

---

[146] Jameson Dempsey, Dawn Damschen, and Steve Augustino, "What to Watch For With the FCC's New Cybersecurity Initiative," *The Telecom Monitor*, June 27, 2014, http://www.telecomlawmonitor.com/2014/06/articles/broadband/what-to-watch-for-with-the-fccs-new-cybersecurity-initiative/.

[147] Ibid.

[148] Bill Hardekopf, "The Big Data Breaches of 2014," *Forbes,* January 13, 2015, http://www.forbes.com/sites/moneybuilder/2015/01/13/the-big-data-breaches-of-2014/.

Photo Removed Due to Copyright Restrictions

Table 1.   Major Data Breaches of 2014[149]

C.   FS-ISAC

The Financial Services Information Sharing Analysis Center (FS-ISAC) is one of several threat information sharing centers that provide two-way sharing of cybersecurity threats between private owners and operators of CI and government agencies. It was established in 1999 as one of the first ISACs created in response to Presidential Decision Directive 63 (PDD-63), which was later superseded by Homeland Security Presidential Directive 7 (HSPD-7). PDD-63 called for the establishment of an information-sharing hub between both public and private sectors to exchange cybersecurity threats, vulnerabilities, risk assessments, and best practices to enhance protection U.S. critical infrastructure.[150] As mentioned in Chapter III, ISACs have been performing as successful examples of cybersecurity information-sharing PPPs.[151] Since inception, membership

---

[149] Data retrieved from Hardekopf, "The Big Data Breaches of 2014."

[150] Financial Services Information Sharing and Analysis Center, "About FS-ISAC," FS-ISAC website, accessed January 3, 2015, https://www.fsisac.com/about.

[151] Cavelty and Suter, "Public-Private Partnerships," 181.

within the FS-ISAC has grown to nearly 5,500 members[152]—not only within the Americas, but globally. In 2013, the ISAC expanded its partnership to participating companies in the regions of Europe, Middle East, and Asia-Pacific.[153] FS-ISAC participation is recommended by the following government agencies: U.S. Treasury, U.S. Secret Service, DHS, and the FSSCC.[154]

Beyond facilitating the sharing of cyber threat information, the FS-ISAC has supported several annual cybersecurity exercises that test the capabilities of financial institutions to respond and recover from cyber-attacks.[155] The most recent exercise was the 5th Annual Cyber Attack Against Payment Processes Simulation (CAPP) held in September 2014, which tested nearly 1,000 participating financial institutions (that utilize payment services) to respond to multiple simulated cyber-attacks in two separate, two-day robust cybersecurity scenarios.[156] In addition to the invaluable experience gained, these CAPP exercises are offered to any institution that utilizes payment services at no cost—allowing small-to-medium sized companies to participate—which ultimately expands the participation potential of the private sector in information-sharing PPPs.

In an effort to address both public and private sector concerns of the timely exchange of cyber-related threat information, the FS-ISAC has adopted the use of two new (DHS driven) automated sharing initiatives that aim to speed up the process of collecting and disseminating cyber-attack data. The Structured Threat Information eXpression (STIX) and Trusted Automated eXchange of Indicator Information (TAXII) programs—initiated and backed by DHS—were designed to help private companies and government agencies streamline (at no cost) their methods of sharing critical cyber threat

---

[152] Financial Services Information Sharing and Analysis Center, "Affiliate Program," FS-ISAC website, accessed January 3, 2015, https://www.fsisac.com/partners/affiliate-programs.

[153] FS-ISAC, "About FS-ISAC."

[154] Ibid.

[155] John Ginovsky, "Cyber Threat." American Bankers Association, *ABA Banking Journal* 104, no. 12 (12, 2012): 27, http://search.proquest.com/docview/1269722356?accountid=12702.

[156] Financial Services Information Sharing and Analysis Center, "FS-ISAC Cyber Attack (against) Payment Processes (CAPP) Exercise," FS-ISAC website, accessed January 10, 2015, https://www.fsisac.com/fs-isac-cyber-attack-against-payment-processes-capp-exercise.

information automatically versus manually.[157] FS-ISAC's continual effort to endorse programs that encourage information-sharing within the banking and financial industry; simplify the methods in which information is shared; and more importantly, address the concerns of both sectors, such as the lack of timely exchange of threat information, only reinforces the value and necessity for private firms to become active participants. Despite such efforts to spur participation, private industry is still finding difficulty in contributing to PPPs.

D.   FINDINGS AND ANALYSIS

In an environment lacking legislation that requires companies to adopt tighter cybersecurity measures, a current evaluation of the effectiveness of information sharing between public and private sector agencies should: first, help identify barriers to establishing cybersecurity PPPs; and second, add value to existing knowledge in cybersecurity issues involving the compromise of U.S. banking and finance infrastructure. Recent testimony from cybersecurity and industry professionals and other empirical research on cybersecurity information-sharing reveal several underlying issues inhibiting public-private cooperation.

In the spring of 2013, the National Telecommunications and Information Administration (NTIA) and NIST requested—under direction from the president—an evaluation of incentives established by DHS that encourage information sharing and adoption of NISTs Framework (still in development at the time). Among the many participants was the Financial Services Sector Coordinating Council (FSSCC) for Critical Infrastructure Protection and Homeland Security—established in 2002 for the purpose of coordinating critical infrastructure protection efforts within the financial sector.[158] In response to NTIA's inquiry, the FSSCC identified several private business concerns with private-public collaboration within the financial sector. The Financial Services Sector

---

[157] Phyllis Schneck, "Hearing on Cyber Security: Prepared Testimony," U.S. Senate Committee on Banking, Housing, and Urban Affairs, December 10, 2014, http://www.banking.senate.gov/public/ index.cfm?FuseAction=Files.View&FileStore_id=990f3741-335b-49be-ad3a-a43475ac41b5.

[158] Financial Services Sector Coordinating Council for Critical Infrastructure Protection and Homeland Security, "Our Mission," FSSCC website, accessed January 29, 2015, http://www.fsscc.org/ fsscc/about/default.jsp.

Coordinating Council (FSSCC) argued that "issues of information sharing, misaligned incentives, criminal penalties and access to government resources" must be resolved if financial institutions are to adopt incentives, such as those outlined in NISTs Framework—a tool designed to improve and encourage information sharing between both public and private divisions across all sectors of CI.[159]

The council found it challenging to offer incentives to private owners and operators of CI within the financial sector to adopt the framework that encourages information-sharing when standards and requirements are unclear.[160] The financial sector is already subject to many regulation requirements, such as federal and state laws; including cybersecurity examination standards derived from the Financial Services Modernization Act of 1999—law that establishes standards for businesses within the finance sector, such as brokerage firms, commercial banks, and insurance companies, to collaborate with one another.[161] Thus, in the absence of clear guidelines that will either become additional requirements or become an entirely new standard, private financial companies will continue to abide by existing regulations, which could deter many private financial firms from collaborating with government agencies.

Another area of concern identified by the FSSCC is the lack of timely exchanges of threat information between both public and private agencies; information that could aid in creating adequate protective measures against malicious online activity.[162] Five years after the GAO reported the same findings (discussed in Chapter I: Literature Review): the same information-sharing issues appear to be troubling the banking and finance CI sector. The FSSCC also conveyed private sector concerns about the balance of incentives and disincentives between attackers and defenders—lack of law enforcement

---

[159] Charles Blauner, "Comments on Incentives to Adopt Improved Cybersecurity Practices: Notice of Inquiry," National Telecommunications and Information Administration, April 29, 2013, 2, http://www.ntia.doc.gov/files/ntia/fsscc_response_-_doc_noi.pdf.

[160] Ibid.

[161] Also known as the Gramm-Leach-Bliley Act; *Gramm-Leach-Bliley Act,* U.S. Government Publishing Office, accessed January 24, 2015, http://www.gpo.gov/fdsys/pkg/PLAW-106publ102/pdf/PLAW-106publ102.pdf.

[162] Blauner, "Comments on Incentives," 2.

prosecuting cyber-criminal activity.[163] While private businesses expect state and federal law enforcement to seek out and prosecute criminals, issues of attribution and the lack of resources to investigate cyber-crimes make it almost impossible to deter cyber criminals or bring them to justice; furthermore, banks and other financial institutions usually sustain losses from cyber-attacks, such as data theft and trade secrets, that are impossible to recover.[164] The imbalance of incentives and disincentives between private financial firms and cyber criminals—coupled with the government's inability to protect and prosecute—could yet be another deterrent to greater private-public collaboration.

While initial concerns of violating anti-trust laws and the FIOA have hindered the establishment of cybersecurity PPPs in earlier years, one constant barrier has continued to be trust issues between the public and private sector. While the majority of literature surrounding cybersecurity PPPs identifies a lack of trust across all sectors of CI as the chief concern among both private and government agencies, the banking and finance industry has begun to develop and experience other concerns. In his testimony before the U.S. Senate Committee on Homeland Security and Governmental Affairs in March 2014, Steven R. Chabinsky expressed his concerns of cybersecurity partnerships between the public and private sector. Among those include: non-disclosure agreements preventing private businesses from sharing threat information with the government; arduous background checks for private firms seeking clearance to classified threat information from the government; larger companies with a global footprint sharing sensitive, government-provided threat information with other security firms abroad; U.S. government agencies sharing newly discovered private business vulnerabilities with other foreign law enforcement and intelligence agencies; and free-riding companies that participate only to collect threat information and to network with other agencies but contribute minimally, or even not at all.[165]

---

163 Blauner, "Comments on Incentives," 3.

164 Ibid.

165 Steven R. Chabinsky, "Strengthening Public-Private Partnerships to Reduce Cyber Risks to our Nation's Critical Infrastructure," Testimony, U.S. Senate Committee on Homeland Security and Governmental Affairs, March 26, 2014, http://www.hsgac.senate.gov/hearings/strengthening-public-private-partnerships-to-reduce-cyber-risks-to-our-nations-critical-infrastructure.

Despite an increase in information flow between the public and private sector in the finance industry, such as the 2009 cybercrime collaboration of the FBI, FS-ISAC, and National Automated Clearinghouse Association (NACHA)—a recent PPP effort aimed at ensuring information exchange between all parties occurs in a timely and tailored manner—private companies have expressed their concerns over the government's uncoordinated influx of bulky and sometimes irrelevant threat information. In other words, government agencies are simply pushing unfiltered data to private agencies that either a) companies already had knowledge of; b) was irrelevant; c) without specific requests from individual clients.[166] Chabinksy's testimony serves as evidence that supports what the GAO found 5 years earlier, when it surveyed five separate CI sectors (noted in Chapter I). Thus, private industry continues to be concerned that government agencies are measuring their information-sharing successes on quantity versus quality, irrespective to the actual utility of threat information, thus serving as another deterrent for private-public cooperation.

In his testimony before the U.S. Senate Committee on Homeland Security and Governmental Affairs in March 2014, Steven R. Chabinsky echoed what the FSSCC had been arguing just one year prior: the unbalanced costs between attackers and defenders.[167] While attackers continue to increasingly penetrate banking and financial networks at a low and sometimes even zero cost, defenders (private industry) continue to see a rise in cybersecurity costs. Private companies are concerned that the government is ineffective in challenging and prosecuting cyber-criminal activity. The recent alleged DDoS attacks from the countries of North Korea and Iran on U.S. financial institutions are an example of how the government has left network security up to the private sector.[168] While private companies continue to focus their resources on reducing vulnerabilities, the government seems to remain disengaged in providing adequate protection, thus increasing security costs to private sector businesses.

---

[166] Chabinsky, "Strengthening Public-Private Partnerships."

[167] Blauner, "Comments on Incentives," 3.

[168] Ibid.

In May 2014, the New York Department of Financial Services (NYDFS) issued its *Report on Cybersecurity in the Banking Sector*, which surveyed 154 financial institutions on the status of their cybersecurity programs and participation in information-sharing partnerships. While the organization's report focused mainly on current cybersecurity programs and barriers within its own organizations, it also discovered, however, that participation in information-sharing partnerships of small- to medium-sized financial institutions (whose assets were between less than $1 billion to $10 billion) was much lower than their larger financial associates (whose assets were greater than $10 billion).[169] Figure 2 illustrates the NYDFS's findings.

Photo Removed Due to Copyright Restrictions

Figure 2.   Financial Institution Participation in Information-sharing[170]

The report noted that while over 60% of larger financial institutions reported participating in information-sharing coalitions, such as the FS-ISAC, fewer than 25% of smaller corporations were—due, in part, to limited financial resources despite the costs for membership in ISACs for smaller financial institutions being relatively low when compared to the benefits of receiving timely physical and cyber threat information.[171]

---

[169] Andrew M. Cuomo, "Report on Cyber Security in the Banking Sector," New York State Department of Financial Services, May 6, 2014, http://www.dfs.ny.gov/about/press2014/pr140505cyber_security.pdf.

[170] Data retrieved from Cuomo, "Report on Cyber Security," 3.

[171] Cuomo, "Report on Cyber Security," 4.

The report concludes that despite a recent increase of private financial firms willing to share threat information and participate in ISACs, there are numerous others that remain on the fence over the fear of exposing any weakness to the public—or worse, to their competitors.[172]

Another challenge to private-public information sharing is found within the Information Technology (IT) sector. As previously noted in Chapter I, cybersecurity issues within the FS sector oftentimes fall into other sectors, such as the IT sector. Frequently, the lines between cybersecurity information sharing within the IT and FS sectors become blurred, such as a network breach of a major retailer that results in financial loss. Thus, it is important to include evidence within the IT sector in this chapter. One of those challenges is the difference in threat perception among government and private industry, despite sharing similar interests. In a 2013 interview, IT-ISAC Executive Director Scott Algeier shared his assessment of cybersecurity information sharing between public-private entities. Algeier did not believe (at the time) that information-sharing was where it needed to be: despite the many successes, such as establishing a baseline risk assessment for the IT sector, which concentrates on low probability-high consequence and high probability-low consequence cyber events, most of these successes are private sector centered rather than joint initiatives. "We have a lot of individual initiatives, but we [do not] have an integrated program," Algeier argued.[173] He observed that one of the primary challenges of private-public cyber information-sharing is how the private IT industry perceives cyber threats. According to Algeier, government agencies view cyber threats and vulnerabilities on a national security level, whereas private companies are primarily concerned about how those cyber threats and vulnerabilities affect business. "Industry and government have common interests, but we look at the threats in a different way," stated Algeier.[174] Although government agencies continue to focus on worst-case scenarios, in Algeier's opinion private companies are not

---

[172] Cuomo, "Report on Cyber Security," 11.

[173] Dan Verton, "Interview: Scott Algeier, Exec. Director, IT-ISAC," *HS Today.US,* January 6, 2013, http://www.hstoday.us/blogs/critical-issues-in-national-cybersecurity/blog/interview-scott-algeier-exec-director-it-isac/045346b3645b76b057089d42d48c8699.html.

[174] Ibid.

convinced these scenarios are the most likely.[175] Due to continual changes in how private industry discloses threat vulnerabilities, such as disclosing weaknesses to stakeholders and customers before sharing with public agencies, information-sharing hubs like the FS and IT-ISACs continually look for new ways to improve threat information sharing; for example, facilitating discussion about cyber-attacks that companies currently experience.[176]

Further challenges to private-public information-sharing were noted in a recent Senate hearing on cybersecurity before the U.S. Senate Committee on Banking, Housing, and Urban Affairs. In December 2014, the Director of Treasury's Office of Critical Infrastructure Protection and Compliance Policy (OCIP), Brian Peretti, briefed the Senate on the current state of cybersecurity efforts between both public and private sectors and the Department of Treasury's role in fostering those relationships. While he identified several reoccurring challenges, such as declassifying threat information for private sector use and increasing efficiency in the information-sharing process, Peretti noted that many private sector companies are still apprehensive in sharing threat information due to the lack of clear legal guidelines.[177] Some government agencies have attempted to ease those concerns. The Department of Justice (DOJ) recently addressed privacy concerns over sharing threat information containing consumer information in a white paper titled: *Sharing Cyberthreat Information Under 18 USC § 2702(a)(3).*[178] The DOJ viewed the Stored Communications Act (SCA)—the law that prohibits sharing consumer information—as a regulation that would permit private companies to share cyber-related threat information with government agencies so long as the data is collective in nature

---

[175] Verton, "Interview: Scott Algeier."

[176] Ibid.

[177] Brian Peretti, "Hearing on Cyber Security: Prepared Testimony," U.S. Senate Committee on Banking, Housing, and Urban Affairs, December 10, 2014, http://www.banking.senate.gov/public/index.cfm?FuseAction=Hearings.Testimony&Hearing_ID=1632c6b0-843f-4b9b-9df2-0a5322324070&Witness_ID=d5e63e2d-46bb-4837-b030-e8f41f31b189.

[178] "Sharing Cyberthreat Information Under 18 USC § 2702(a)(3)," Department of Justice, May 9, 2014, http://www.justice.gov/criminal/cybercrime/docs/guidance-for-ecpa-issue-5-9-2014.pdf.

and does not single out any one individual.[179] Despite such attempts to read between the legal lines, many private companies are still reluctant to share data with the government due to fears of public disclosure (e.g., the Snowden revelations), preventing private companies from conducting their own damage control and finding a resolution before public exposure.[180] This is concerning to private financial firms in relation to exposure due to the large pool of government actors involved: the Federal Trade Commission (FTC), Securities and Exchange Commission (SEC), Department of Justice (DOJ), National Security Agency (NSA), and U.S. CYBERCOM.[181] Each of these agencies has a unique role in regulating cybersecurity, which only increases the probability of an unintentional or accidental exposure.[182]

E.   SUMMARY

Both private and public institutions that operate within the finance CI sector continue to depend on the security of our nation's financial networks for trade and communication. Increasing cyber-attacks to banks, financial institutions, and individuals from criminals, hactivists, and even states—primarily China and Iran—require the use of information sharing PPPs to increase security and efficiency in both public and private networks, and help close the gap in government and private sector cooperation. For 15 years, the FS-ISAC has continued to develop ways and means of facilitating cybersecurity information sharing between government agencies and private companies; most notably, their annual CAPP exercises that test the resiliency of private companies to respond to multiple cyber-attacks, and endorsement of the STIX and TAXII programs designed to speed up the information sharing process. The FSSCC and NIST have also made notable strides in fostering the creation of PPPs to enhance cybersecurity information sharing within the financial sector.

---

[179] Kimberly Peretti and Dennig, Lou, "Don't Be Afraid of Cybersecurity Information Sharing," Corporate Counsel, September 9, 2014, http://www.corpcounsel.com/id=1202669281129/Dont-Be-Afraid-of-Cybersecurity-Information-Sharing?slreturn=20150109122554.

[180] Judith H. Germano, "Cybersecurity Partnerships: A New Era of Public-Private Collaboration," New York University School of Law Center on Law and Security, October 2014, 4, http://www.lawandsecurity.org/Portals/0/Documents/Cybersecurity.Partnerships.pdf.

[181] Ibid.

[182] Ibid.

This chapter assessed the current challenges facing the establishment of PPPs to advance cyber information sharing within the finance sector of critical infrastructure. Those concerns include: lack of trust, lack of incentives, and timely exchange of threat information; differences in threat perception; free-riding institutions that only collect rather than share threat information; government agencies pushing useless, unfiltered data; limited resources (assets) for smaller companies; and fears of legal and reputation damages due to public disclosure. The evidence found in this case study suggests that there are several other explanations beyond the original three hypotheses proposed in Chapter I. The validation of the original three and the additional explanations are discussed in the next chapter. Despite the significant hurdles facing both sides in collaborating, the recent surge in cyber-attacks targeting U.S. critical infrastructure should be incentive enough for companies to get onboard with the PPP concept. It is reasonable to argue, based on evidence presented in this chapter, that the efforts from the FS-ISAC, IT-ISAC, FSSCC, and NIST, are not only addressing the concerns of private companies in the finance industry, but also making positive strides towards breaking down barriers between public and private information sharing.

THIS PAGE INTENTIONALLY LEFT BLANK

V. CONCLUSION

A. SYNOPSIS

Chapter I introduced the topic of cybersecurity within the public-private sector to set up the major thesis question: Why do cybersecurity information-sharing problems exist between government agencies and private companies? It also established the importance of the research; explored the prevalent literature on cybersecurity information-sharing within the public and private sector; provided three potential hypotheses that best explain why barriers to public and private cooperation in cyber information-sharing exist today; and identified the banking and finance CI sector as the most promising case study to validate the three explanations. As stated in Chapter I, the banking and finance sector has not only experienced a significant increase in cyber-attacks—to include identity theft and breaches of major retail companies—but also has the potential to suffer the most catastrophic damage to the nation's security, economy, and way of life. Thus, this thesis recognized the finance industry as the most prominent sector in which to examine and gather new evidence.

Chapter II provided a background of the more recent cyber-related attacks across various sectors of CI to further establish the importance and urgency of cybersecurity information-sharing between the public and private sectors. The chapter also offered a brief description of the most recent controversial cybersecurity policies and legislation dilemmas relevant to this research—including CISA, EO 13636, PPD-21, and the 2013 NIPP; and DHS and NIST's response to various cybersecurity requirements ordered under EO 13636—such as NIST's Cybersecurity Framework and DHS's C^{e}VP program.

Chapter III introduced the concept of cybersecurity public-private partnerships (PPP) and identified several factors that promote, challenge, and limit the establishment of, and agency participation in, cybersecurity information-sharing partnerships to defend against cyber-related threats. This chapter identified and discussed current cybersecurity PPPs in action—such as the Enduring Security Framework (the collaboration of several major IT and defense companies that meet several times annually to discuss current cyber threats and best practices); the National Cyber Forensics and Training Alliance (public-private effort that supports the timely exchange of up-to-date cyber threats and cyber-related crimes that occur within sectors, including the finance sector); and the major public-private effort that went into developing NIST's Cybersecurity Framework 1.0. While information-sharing between both sectors has improved, several challenges, such as lack of trust, legal barriers, and failed expectations, continue to hinder the success of PPPs in cybersecurity.

Chapter IV explored the banking and financial CI sector to identify and assess the current challenges facing the establishment of PPPs to advance cyber information-sharing between the government and private companies. Lack of trust and incentives, timely exchange of threat information, varying threat perceptions, free-riding, sharing of useless or unfiltered data, limited resources for smaller businesses, and fears of legal liability and damage to company image were the common themes found within the financial sector that continue to inhibit the success of information-sharing PPPs. This evidence not only validates the three hypotheses introduced in Chapter I, it also reveals several other explanations that are discussed in the next section.

B.   HYPOTHESIS TEST

The three proposed hypotheses will now be tested based on evidence provided in Chapters III and IV in an effort to answer the major research question of why information-sharing problems exist between government agencies and private companies. While this evidence helps validate the three explanations introduced in Chapter I, it also reveals several others; thus, those additional findings are provided following validation of the initial three hypotheses.

1.   Hypothesis One:

Participation in PPPs is less likely to occur when either side fails to share cyber-related information in a timely and accurate manner.

This explanation assumes that both government and private businesses expect these to be the minimum requirements for participation in a cybersecurity information-sharing alliance. While earlier literature (discussed in Chapter I) was used to arrive at this explanation, evidence found in Chapter IV equally supports this hypothesis.

a. *Timely Exchange of Threat Information*

Despite recent and ongoing efforts of PPPs, such as FS-ISAC's automated sharing initiatives, STIX and TAXII;[183] and NCFTA's cybercrime network,[184] to increase the timely exchange of cyber-related threat information, further evidence found in Chapter IV corroborates the claim of this first hypothesis. One example is the FSSCC's finding that both public and private companies within the banking and finance sector lack timely sharing of cyber-related threat information that could facilitate the creation of adequate protective programs against malicious online activity.[185] Another example is found in Steven Chabinsky's testimony that despite the recent increase in information flow between both sectors within the finance industry, private companies continue to express concern over the government's push of uncoordinated, bulky, irrelevant, and unsolicited threat information.[186] Private firms worry that the government is more concerned about quantity versus quality without regard to the actual utility of the information being shared. Further support of this hypothesis is found in Manuel Suter's cybersecurity briefing—held in Zurich, Switzerland in 2010—in which he identified misplaced expectations between both government and private companies as one of several major challenges facing cybersecurity information sharing PPPs aimed at protecting CI.[187]

2. Hypothesis Two

Private companies feel threatened by cybersecurity regulations and standards that increase security costs, risk the loss of market share, and lack incentives, thus decreasing the likelihood of PPP participation.

---

[183] Schneck, "Hearing on Cyber Security."

[184] Plesco and Schneck, "Criminal Public-Private Partnerships."

[185] Blauner, "Comments on Incentives," 2.

[186] Chabinsky, "Strengthening Public-Private Partnerships."

[187] Suter, "Unpacking Public-Private Partnerships."

This hypothesis assumes that companies are less likely to share cyber-related information when government regulations and standards create at least one of the three conditions: security cost increase; risk to market share; and lack of incentives. While earlier evidence provided in the literature review aided in producing this hypothesis, further evidence found in both Chapters III and IV equally supports this second explanation. The three identified conditions in this hypothesis are discussed below separately.

a.   *Security Cost Increase*

Both Chabinsky and the FSSCC found that private companies are concerned with the unbalanced costs between attackers and defenders.[188] While attackers continue to increasingly penetrate banking and financial networks at a low and sometimes even zero cost, Chabinsky argued that private companies continue to see a rise in cybersecurity costs. For example, recent DDoS attacks from other nation states, such as North Korea and Iran, has the private sector worried that big government is leaving individual companies on their own to defend against such attacks.[189] Private companies are forced to focus their resources on reducing vulnerabilities while the government remains disengaged, thus increasing security costs to private businesses.[190]

b.   *Risk to Market Share*

The NYDFS's *Report on Cybersecurity in the Banking Sector* found that despite the recent increase of private financial firms willing to share threat information and participate in information-sharing PPPs, such as the FS-ISAC, numerous private companies remain reluctant due to fears of exposing weakness, not only to consumers but also to other competing companies within the finance industry.[191] Further evidence suggests that many private companies are still reluctant to share data with the government due to fears of public disclosure, such as the recent Edward Snowden revelations. Public

---

[188] Blauner, "Comments on Incentives," 3.

[189] Ibid.

[190] Ibid.

[191] Cuomo, "Report on Cyber Security," 11.

leaks, such as this, prevent individual private companies from conducting damage control and establishing resolution prior to public exposure, thus resulting in a higher risk of market share loss to competitors.[192] Additionally, the risk of market share loss due to unintentional or accidental exposure increases significantly when multiple government agencies, such as the FTC, SEC, DOJ, U.S. CYBERCOM, and NSA, become involved in regulating cybersecurity, further preventing private companies from participating in PPPs that share cyber-threat information.[193]

c.   *Lack of Incentives*

While ISACs facilitate the collection, evaluation, and dissemination of cyber threat information, problems such as free riding—companies that participate only to collect threat information while making no contribution—often result from the lack of adequate incentives.[194] A major limitation to information-sharing PPPs, such as the FS-ISAC, is that most are voluntary and lack the necessary incentives to encourage participation; in other words, information shared is limited to information received.[195] Further evidence, provided by the FSSCC, suggests that private companies feel that a lack of criminal penalties and limited access to government resources must be resolved if private financial institutions are to adopt incentives, such as those defined in NIST's framework—designed to improve and encourage information sharing between both public and private entities across all sectors of CI.[196] The FSSCC also found that offering incentives to private owners and operators within the financial sector to adopt the framework is a major challenge when standards and requirements are unclear.[197] Further discussion of NIST's Framework is provided in Chapter II. The FSSCC also argued that the balance of incentives and disincentives between attackers and defenders also concerns

---

[192] Germano, "Cybersecurity Partnerships," 4.

[193] Ibid.

[194] McNally, "Improving Public-Private Sector Cooperation," 151–2.

[195] Ibid.

[196] Blauner, "Comments on Incentives," 2.

[197] Ibid.

private companies.[198] Private businesses expect law enforcement to prosecute cyber-criminal activity; however, issues of attribution and lack of resources to investigate cyber-crimes have made it difficult to deter cyber criminals. Furthermore, financial institutions have sustained unrecoverable losses from cyber-attacks, such as data theft and trade secrets.[199] The imbalance of incentives and disincentives between private financial firms and cyber criminals—coupled with the government's inability to protect and prosecute—continue to deter private-public collaboration.

3. Hypothesis Three

Small- to medium-sized private sector companies lack the necessary resources to participate in information-sharing cybersecurity PPPs.

While the evidence presented in this thesis to support this hypothesis is significantly less than the first two, it is worth noting the findings provided in Chapter IV that help support this claim.

a. *Small- to Medium-Sized Companies Lack Resources*

Despite the lack of substantial evidence on small-to-medium sized financial companies' ability or willingness to participate in cybersecurity information-sharing PPPs, the NYDFS's *Report on Cybersecurity in the Banking Sector* is one respectable source. As noted in Chapter IV, the report found that fewer than 25% of smaller corporations were participating in information-sharing partnerships, such as the FS-ISAC, due to limited financial resources—despite the costs for membership of most ISACs for smaller financial institutions (whose assets were less than $1 billion) being relatively low compared to the benefits of receiving timely physical and cyber threat information.[200] Figure 2 in Chapter IV illustrates the NYDFS's findings and compares smaller companies with their larger associates. It is also worth noting that while recent cybersecurity exercises, such as the FS-ISAC's annual Cyber Attack Against Payment Processes Simulation (CAPP), have attracted many small- to medium-sized companies to

---

[198] Blauner, "Comments on Incentives," 3.

[199] Ibid.

[200] Cuomo, "Report on Cyber Security," 4.

66

participate at no cost—potentially expanding participation of private firms in information-sharing PPPs—this thesis found no evidence or data to support this claim.[201] Further research into individual financial firms could reveal additional data, which was outside the scope of this thesis.

4. Additional Explanations

In addition to the three hypotheses tested above, this thesis found several other common and credible explanations as to why barriers exist between government agencies and private companies within the financial sector. The likely barriers identified in both Chapters III (Cybersecurity PPPs) and IV (Financial Sector Case Study) include:

- **Lack of trust**

- **Fears of legal and reputation damages due to public disclosure**

- **Diverging interests, such as differences in threat perception**

- **Free-riding due to volunteer nature of information-sharing**

- **Limited resources for smaller companies**

Although the challenges and limitations to establishing and employing information-sharing PPPs to effectively counter cyber threats are numerous, this thesis found these to be the most prominent concerns among public and private sector entities within the banking and financial CI sector.

C. CONSIDERATIONS FOR FURTHER RESEARCH

While this thesis explored cybersecurity issues between the government and private sector utilizing only published information (such as academic journals, interviews, opinion pieces, and government reports), future research that includes personal interviews with Executives, Information Officers, and IT specialists of major private companies could reveal additional barriers that inhibit public-private cooperation. To ensure the credibility of these sources, every effort should be made to avoid source

---

[201] Ginovsky, "Cyber Threat," 27.

anonymity. Additionally, while this thesis focused exclusively on the banking and finance CI sector, future research could include a cross-sector comparison among other similar CI sectors, such as the IT and communications sector, in an effort to identify the similarities and differences of how each sector deals with information-sharing problems. Similarly, an evaluation of how the several different ISACs foster information-sharing between the government and private sector companies could add value to the existing body of knowledge on cybersecurity issues between the government and private sector.

LIST OF REFERENCES

Bataller, Erik. "Cyber Partnerships." *InformationWeek* no. 1295 (Mar 28, 2011): 21–24. http://search.proquest.com/docview/860133412?accountid=12702.

Beeson, Ben, Gerald Ferguson, and Mark Weatherford. "Implementation of the Cybersecurity Executive Order." Slide 6, November 13, 2013. http://chertoffgroup.com/events.php.

Bennett, Ashley. "Cybersecurity Expert Explains Importance of NCCIP Act." *Government Security News*, February 11, 2014. Assessed May 30, 2014. http://www.gsnmagazine.com/article/40197/cybersecurity_expert_explains_impor tance_nccip_act.

Blauner, Charles. "Comments on Incentives to Adopt Improved Cybersecurity Practices: Notice of Inquiry." National Telecommunications and Information Administration, April 29, 2013. http://www.ntia.doc.gov/files/ntia/fsscc_ response_-_doc_noi.pdf.

Brennan, John. "Time to Protect Against Dangers of Cyberattack." *The Washington Post*, April 15, 2012. http://www.washingtonpost.com/opinions/time-to-protect-against-dangers-ofcyberattack/2012/ 04/15/gIQAdJP8JT_story.html.

Busch, Nathan E., and Austen D. Givens. "Public-Private Partnerships in Homeland Security: Opportunities and Challenges." *Homeland Security Affairs* 8, no. 1 (2012). http://search.proquest. com/docview/1266365905?accountid=12702.

Business Software Alliance, et al. "Improving our Nation's Cybersecurity Through the Public-Private Partnership: White Paper," March 8, 2011, 17. https://cdt.org/files/ pdfs/ 20110308_cbyersec_ paper.pdf.

Cavelty, Myriam Dunn, and Manuel Suter. "Public-Private Partnerships are no Silver Bullet: An Expanded Governance model for Critical Infrastructure Protection." *International Journal of Critical Infrastructure Protection* Vol. 4, no. 2 (March, 2009): 179–187. doi:10.1016/j.ijep.2009.08.006.

Cellucci, Thomas. "Innovative Public-Private Partnerships: Pathway to Effectively Solving Problems." Department of Homeland Security, July 2010. http://www.dhs.gov/xlibrary/ assets/st_innovative_public_private_partnerships_ 0710_version_2.pdf.

Chabinsky, Steven R. "Strengthening Public-Private Partnerships to Reduce Cyber Risks to our Nation's Critical Infrastructure." Testimony. U.S. Senate Committee on Homeland Security and Governmental Affairs, March 26, 2014. http://www.hsgac.senate.gov/hearings/strengthening-public-private-partnerships-to-reduce-cyber-risks-to-our-nations-critical-infrastructure.

Chinn, Veronica A., Lee T. Furches, and Barian A. Woodward. "Information- Sharing with the Private Sector." National Defense University Press, April 1, 2014. http://ndupress.ndu.edu/Media/News/NewsArticleView/tabid/7849/Article/8464/jfq-73-information-sharing-with-the-private-sector.aspx.

Comey, James B. "The FBI and the Private Sector: Closing the Gap in Cyber Security." Speech, February 26, 2014. http://www.fbi.gov/news/speeches/the-fbi-and-the-private-sector-closing-the-gap-in-cyber-security.

"Critical Infrastructure Cyber Community Voluntary Program." United States Computer Emergency Readiness Team. Department of Homeland Security. Assessed May 27, 2014, http://www.us-cert.gov/ccubedvp.

"Critical Infrastructure Sectors." Department of Homeland Security. Accessed December, 15 2014, http://www.dhs.gov/critical-infrastructure-sectors.

Critical Infrastructure Partnership Advisory Council (CIPAC). "Cross Sector Enduring Security Framework (ESF) Operations Working Group Agenda." Department of Homeland Security. Accessed, January, 15 2015. http://www.dhs.gov/sites/default/files/publications/cipac-cs-esf-ops-agenda-09–17–14–508_0.pdf.

Cuomo, Andrew M. "Report on Cyber Security in the Banking Sector." New York State Department of Financial Services, May 6, 2014. http://www.dfs.ny.gov/about/press2014/pr140505cyber_ security.pdf.

Curran, John. "Chertoff: Cybersecurity Requires More Public-Private Cooperation." *Cybersecurity Policy Report* (May 02, 2011): 1. http://search.proquest.com/docview/867525563?accountid=12702.

Dempsey Jameson, Dawn Damschen, and Steve Augustino. "What to Watch For With the FCC's New Cybersecurity Initiative." *The Telecom Monitor*, June 27, 2014. http://www.telecomlawmonitor.com/ 2014/06/articles/broadband/what-to-watch-for-with-the-fccs-new-cybersecurity-initiative/.

Department of Treasury. *Department of the Treasury FY 2014–2017 Strategic Plan*. 32. http://www.treasury.gov/about/budget-performance/strategic-plan/Documents/2014–2017_U.S._ TreasuryStrategicPlan.pdf.

Dutta, Amitava, and Kevin McCrohan. "Management's Role in Information Security in a Cyber Economy." California Management Review 45, no. 1 (Fall, 2002): 67–87. http://search.proquest.com/ docview/215864793?accountid=12702.

Egan, Matt. "Banks Deploy Shields to Block New Wave of Cyber Attacks." Fox Business, July 31, 2013. http://www.foxbusiness.com/technology/2013/07/31/ banks-deploy-shields-to-block-new-wave-cyber-attacks/.

Engleman, Eric, and Jonathan D. Salant. "U.S. Cybersecurity Policy Draws Interest From Companies, Lobbyists." *The Washington Post,* March 24, 2013. http://www.washingtonpost.com/business/ economy/us-cybersecurity-policy-draws-interest-from-companies-lobbyists/2013/03/24/ 916a79f2–9271–11e2-bdea-e32ad90da 239_story.html.

Executive Order no. 13636. *Improving Critical Infrastructure Cybersecurity*. DCPD-2013000 91, February 19, 2013. http://www.gpo.gov/fdsys/pkg/FR-2013–02–19/pdf/2013–03915.pdf.

"Fact Sheet: Executive Order 13636 and Presidential Policy Directive (PPD)-21." Department of Homeland Security, March 2013. http://www.dhs.gov/publication/ fact-sheet-eo-13636-improving-critical-infrastructure-cybersecurity-and-ppd-21-critical.

Financial Services Information Sharing and Analysis Center. "About FS-ISAC." FS-ISAC website. Accessed January 3, 2015. https://www.fsisac.com/about.

———. "Affiliate Program." FS-ISAC website. Accessed January 3, 2015. https://www.fsisac.com/partners/affiliate-programs.

———. "FS-ISAC Cyber Attack (against) Payment Processes (CAPP) Exercise." FS-ISAC website. Accessed January 10, 2015. https://www.fsisac.com/fs-isac-cyber-attack-against-payment-processes-capp-exercise.

Financial Services Sector Coordinating Council for Critical Infrastructure Protection and Homeland Security. "Our Mission." FSSCC website. Accessed January 29, 2015. http://www.fsscc.org/fsscc/ about/default.jsp.

Fisher, Eric A., Edward C. Liu, John Rollins, and Catherine A Theohary. "The 2013 Cybersecurity Executive Order: Overview and Considerations for Congress." Congressional Research Service, March 1, 2013. http://www2.gwu.edu/~nsarchiv/ NSAEBB/NSAEB B424/docs/Cyber-089.pdf.

"Framework for Improving Critical Infrastructure Cybersecurity: Version 1.0." National Institute Standards and Technology, February 12, 2014. http://www.nist.gov/ cyberframework/upload/ cybersecurity-framework-021214.pdf.

Germano, Judith H. "Cybersecurity Partnerships: A New Era of Public-Private Collaboration." New York University School of Law Center on Law and Security, October 2014. http://www.lawandsecurity.org/Portals/0/Documents/ Cybersecurity.Partnerships.pdf.

Ginovsky, John. "Cyber Threat." American Bankers Association. *ABA Banking Journal* 104, no. 12 (12, 2012): 24–28. http://search.proquest.com/docview/ 1269722356?accountid=12702.

Gjelton, Tom. "Cyber Briefings 'Scare the Bejeezus' Out of CEOs." NPR web, May 9, 2012. http://www.npr.org/2012/05/09/152296621/cyber-briefings-scare-the-bejeezus-out-of-ceos.

Gramm-Leach-Bliley Act. U.S. Government Publishing Office. Accessed January 24, 2015. http://www.gpo.gov/fdsys/pkg/PLAW-106publ102/pdf/ PLAW-106publ102.pdf.

Hardekopf, Bill. "The Big Data Breaches of 2014." *Forbes,* January 13, 2015. http://www.forbes.com/sites/moneybuilder/2015/01/13/the-big-data-breaches-of-2014/.

Hare, Forrest B. "The Interdependent Nature of National Cyber Security: Motivating Private Action for a Public Good" (PhD diss., George Mason University, 2010), 155, Dudley Knox Inter Library Loan: 129484.

Hight, Elizabeth A. "Forging A Public-private Partnership for Cybersecurity: Government, Private Sector Collaboration Key to Forward-looking Security." Washington Technology, April 30, 2013. http://washingtontechnology.com/ articles/2013/04/30/insights-hight-cyber-collaboration.aspx.

Huergo, Jennifer. "NIST Releases Cybersecurity Framework Version 1.0." NIST, February 12, 2014. http:// www.nist.gov/itl/csd/launch-cybersecurity-framework-021214.cfm.

Johnson, Nicole Blake. "The Cybersecurity Framework's Role in the Heartbleed Saga." *Fedtech Magazine,* July 3, 2014. http://www.fedtechmagazine.com/ article/2014/07/cybersecurity-frameworks-role-heartbleed-saga.

Kaiser, Tiffany. "DHS: Cyber Attacks Against U.S. Infrastructure Increased by 52 Percent in 2012." Daily Tech, January 10, 2013. http://www.dailytech.com/DHS+Cyber+ Attacks+Against+U.S.+Infrastructure+Increased+by+52+Percent+in+2012/article 29632.htm.

Kash, Wyatt. "Why Businesses Can't Ignore U.S. Cybersecurity Framework." *Information Week,* February 14, 2014. http://www.informationweek.com/government/ cybersecurity/why-businesses-cant-ignore-us-cybersecurity-framework/d/did/ 1113838.

Kitten, Tracey. "DDoS: Attackers Announce Phase 4." Bank Info Security. Information Security Media Group, July 23, 2013. http://www.bankinfosecurity.com/ddos-attackers-announce-phase-4-a-5929/op-1.

Kelley, Diana. "Application Security Risk Management and the NIST Cybersecurity Framework." Security Intelligence, March 3, 2014. http://securityintelligence.com/nist-cybersecurity-framework-application-security-risk-management/#.VBSx1xLn_IV.

Korns Stephen W., and Joshua E. Kastenberg. "Georgia's Cyber Left Hook." *Parameters* 38, no. 4 (2009): 60–76, Proquest Research Library (198032208).

Lynn, William J. "Defending a New Domain: The Pentagon's Cyberstrategy." *Foreign Affairs* 89, no. 5 (September 2010): 97–108. http://search.proquest.com/docview/815278494?accountid=12702.

McCain, Lohn, Kay Hutchison, and Saxby Chambliss. "No Cybersecurity Executive Order, Please." *The Wall Street Journal*, Sept 4, 2012. http://www.mccain.senate.gov/public/ index.cfm/opinion-editorials?ID=c50 83e37–061e-ac3f-8e9b-2594e 43f9d2c.

McCaul, Michael. "Hardening Our Defenses Against Cyberwarfare." *The Wall Street Journal*, March 5, 2013. http://online.wsj.com/news/articles/SB1000142412788 732466240457833686250876342.

McNally, Julie. "Improving Public-Private Sector Cooperation on Cyber Event Reporting."Academic Conferences International Limited, 2013. http://search.proquest.com/docview/1549246645?accountid=12702.

Mueller, Robert S. "Remarks prepared for delivery." RSA Cyber Security Conference, Federal Bureau of Investigation, March 1, 2012. http://www.fbi.gov/news/speeches/combating-threats-in-the-cyber-world-outsmarting-terrorists-hackers-and-spies.

Nakashima, Ellen. "On Cybersecurity Bill, Battle Lines Forming." *The Washington Post,* February 17, 2012. http://www.washingtonpost.com/blogs/checkpoint-washington/ post/divisions-erupt-over-cybersecurity-bill/2012/02/17gIQAG 348IR_blog.html.

National Infrastructure Protection Plan (NIPP 2013): Partnering to Enhance Protection and Resiliency. U.S. Department of Homeland Security, (Washington, DC: 2009). http://www.dhs.gov/sites/default/files/publications/NIPP%202013_Partnering%20 for%20Critical%20Infrastructure%20Security%20and%20Resilience_508_0.pdf.

National Institute of Standards and Technology. "6th Cybersecurity Framework Workshop." U.S. Department of Commerce. Last updated September 12, 2014. http://www.nist.gov/cyberframework/6th-cybersecurity-framework-workshop-october-29–30–2014.cfm."

———. "Cybersecurity Framework—Workshops and Events." U.S. Department of Commerce. Last updated September 12, 2014. http://www.nist.gov/ cyberframework /cybersecurity-framework-events.cfm.

———. "NIST Roadmap for Improving Critical Infrastructure Cybersecurity." U.S. Department of Commerce, February 12, 2014. http://www.nist.gov/ cyberframework/upload/ roadmap-021214.pdf.

Neustar Commends the U.S. Government for Encouraging Public-Private Partnerships to Meet Cyber Security Challenges." *Business Wire*, Feb 22, 2012. http://search.proquest.com/docview/922610532?accountid=12702.

Obama, Barack. "Taking the Cyberattack Threat Seriously." *The Wall Street Journal,* July 19, 2012. http://online.wsj.com/news/articles/SB10000872396390444330904577535492 693044650.

Peacock, Nelson. "Cybersecurity Could be the Next Bipartisan Breakthrough." *The Hill*, January 22, 2014. Assessed May 30, 2014. http://thehill.com/blogs/congress-blog/technology/196026-cybersecurity-could-be-the-next-bipartisan-breakthrough.

Peretti, Brian. "Hearing on Cyber Security: Prepared Testimony." U.S. Senate Committee on Banking, Housing, and Urban Affairs, December 10, 2014. http://www.banking.senate.gov/public/ index.cfm?FuseAction=Hearings. Testimony&Hearing_ID=1632c6b0–843f-4b9b-9df2–0a5322324070 &Witness_ID=d5e63e2d-46bb-4837-b030-e8f41f31b189.

Peretti, Kimberly, and Lou Dennig. "Don't Be Afraid of Cybersecurity Information Sharing." Corporate Counsel, September 9, 2014. http://www.corpcounsel.com/ id=1202669281129/Dont-Be-Afraid-of-Cybersecurity-Information-Sharing? slreturn=20150109122554.

Peterson, Andrea, and Sean Pool. "Timeline: U.S. Security Policy in Context: A Look at President Obama's Latest Executive Order and the Policies that Preceded It." Science Progress, February 13, 2013. http://scienceprogress.org/2013/02/u-s-cybersecurity-policy-in-context/.

Plesco, Ron, and Phyllis Schneck. "Criminal Public-Private Partnerships: Why can't we do that?" *Georgetown Journal of International Affairs* (Fall, 2011): 151–154. http://search.proquest.com/docview/911784343?accountid=12702.

Powner, David A. *Critical Infrastructure Protection: Key Private and Public Cyber Expectations Need to be Consistently Addressed.* United States Government Accountability Office, 2010, 7, http://search.proquest.com/docview/ 831086945?accountid=12702.

"Rachel Nyswander Thomas," bio, Direct Marketing Association website, http://thedma.org/ dma/rachel-nyswander-thomas/.

Riddell, Kelly. "Ex-FBI Official: Intel Agencies Don't Share Cyber threats that Endanger Companies." *The Washington Times,* May 11, 2014. http://www.washingtontimes.com/news/2014/may/11/ intel-agencies-dont-share-cyber-threats-that-could/?page=all.

Rosenzweig, Paul. "Cybersecurity Information Sharing and the Freedom of Information Act: Statement before the Committee on the Judiciary United States Senate." The Heritage Foundation, March 14, 2012. http://www.heritage.org/research/ testimony/2012/03/cybersecurity-information-sharing-and-the-freedom-of-information-act.

Sanger, David E., and Eric Schmitt. "Rise is Seen in Cyberattacks Targeting U.S. Infrastructure." *The New York Times,* July 26, 2012. http://www.nytimes.com/ 2012/07/27/us/ cyberattacks-are-up-national-security-chief-says.html.

Schmitt, Michael N. *Tallinn Manual On the International Law Applicable to Cyber Warfare: Prepared By the International Group of Experts At the Invitation of the NATO Cooperative Cyber Defence Centre of Excellence.* (New York: Cambridge University Press, 2013).

Schmidt, Michael. "New Interest in Hacking as Threat to Security." *The New York Times*, March 13, 2012. http://www.nytimes.com/2012/03/14/us/new-interest-in-hacking-as-threat-to-us-security.html?_r=0.

Schneck, Phyllis. "Hearing on Cyber Security: Prepared Testimony." U.S. Senate Committee on Banking, Housing, and Urban Affairs, December 10, 2014. http://www.banking.senate.gov/public/index.cfm?FuseAction=Files.View& FileStore_id=990f3741–335b-49be-ad3a-a43475ac41b5.

"Seven Keys to Success: Public-Private Partnerships Defined." The National Council for Public-Private Partnerships. Accessed January 3, 2015. http://www.ncppp.org/ ppp-basics/7-keys/.

"Sharing Cyberthreat Information Under 18 USC § 2702(a)(3)." Department of Justice, May 9, 2014. http://www.justice.gov/criminal/cybercrime/docs/guidance-for-ecpa-issue-5–9-2014.pdf.

"Significant Cyber Events." Center for Strategic and International Studies, last modified March 10, 2014. http://csis.org/files/publication/140310_Significant_Cyber_Incidents_Since_2006.pdf.

Smith, Gerry. "Senate Won't Vote on CISPA, Deals Blow Controversial Cyber Bill." *Huffington Post*, April 25, 2013. http://www.huffingtonpost.com/2013/04/25/ cispa-cyber-bill_n_3158221. html.

Stewart, Geoffrey T., Ramesh Kolluru, and Mark Smith. "Leveraging Public-Private Partnerships to Improve Community Resilience in Times of Disaster." International Journal of Physical Distribution & Logistics Management 39, no. 5 (2009): 343–364. http://search.proquest.com/docview/232592275?accountId= 12702.

Stiennon, Richard. "PPD-21: Extreme Risk Management Gone Bad." *Forbes*, February 14, 2013. http:// www.forbes.com/sites/richardstiennon/2013/02/14/ppd-21-extreme-risk-management-gone-bad/.

Suter, Manuel. "Unpacking Public-Private Partnerships: Identifying Differences, Challenges and Practices of Collaboration in Cyber Security." George Mason University International Cyber Center. Accessed January 10, 2015. http://www.internationalcybercenter.org/workshops/cs-ga-2010–1/cs-ga-2010/msuter.

"The Cyber Threat—Planning for the Way Ahead." Federal Bureau of Investigation, February 19, 2013. http://www.fbi.gov/news/stories/2013/february/the-cyber-threat-planning-for-the-way-ahead/the-cyber-threat-planning-for-the-way-ahead.

Thomas, Rachel Nyswander. "Securing Cyberspace Through Public-Private Partnership: A Comparative Analysis of Partnership Models." May 2012. Last updated August 2013. http://csis.org/files/ publication/130819_ tech_summary.pdf.

Tracy, Ryan. "Cybersecurity Legislation Gets Push From Financial Firms." *The Wall Street Journal*, Law Blog, November 13, 2013. http://blogs.wsj.com/law/2013/ 11/13/cybersecurity-legislation-gets-push-from-financial-firms/.

"U.S. Cyber Command Fact Sheet." U.S. Strategic Command. Accessed January 8, 2015. http://www.stratcom.mil/factsheets/2/Cyber_Command/.

Verton, Dan. "Interview: Scott Algeier, Exec. Director, IT-ISAC." *HS Today.U.S.*, January 6, 2013. http://www.hstoday.us/blogs/critical-issues-in-national-cybersecurity/blog/interview-scott-algeier-exec-director-it-isac/045346b3645b76b057089d42d48c8699.html.

Wagstaff, Keith. "The Breakdown: Who Supports CISPA and Who Doesn't." *Time*, April 30, 2012. http://techland.time.com/2012/04/30/the-breakdown-who-supports-cispa-and-who-doesnt/.

Weisman, Aly. "A Timeline of the Crazy Events in the Sony Hacking Scandal." *Business Insider*, December 9, 2014. http://www.businessinsider.com/sony-cyber-hack-timeline-2014–12.

White House, The. "Presidential Policy Directive/PPD-21: Critical Infrastructure Security and Resilience." U.S. General Services Administration, February 12, 2013. http://www.gsa.gov/portal/mediaId/ 176571/fileName/ATTCH_2_-_PPD-21. action.

Whittaker, Zach. "Failed Twice, Revived Again: CISPA Returns Despite Concerns Over Privacy, Data Sharing." ZDNet, April 30, 2014. http://www.zdnet.com/failed-twice-revived-again-cispa-returns-despite-concerns-over-privacy-data-sharing-7000028943/.